TRAVELLERS

HAWAII

By
ALISON LEMER

Written by Alison Lemer
Original photography by Alison Lemer

Published by Thomas Cook Publishing
A division of Thomas Cook Tour Operations Limited.
Company registration no. 1450464 England
The Thomas Cook Business Park, 9 Coningsby Road,
Peterborough PE3 8SB, United Kingdom
E-mail: sales@thomascook.com, Tel: + 44 (0) 1733 416477
www.thomascookpublishing.com

Produced by Cambridge Publishing Management Limited
Burr Elm Court, Main Street, Caldecote CB23 7NU

ISBN: 978-1-84157-902-3

First edition © 2008 Thomas Cook Publishing
Text © Thomas Cook Publishing
Maps © Thomas Cook Publishing/PCGraphics (UK) Limited

Series Editor: Maisie Fitzpatrick
Production/DTP: Steven Collins

Printed and bound in Italy by Printer Trento

Cover photography: Front L-R: © Corbis/Photolibrary.com; © Walter
Bibikow/Photolibrary.com; © Giovanni Simeone/SIME-4Corners Images.
Back L-R: © Rita Ariyoshi/Photolibrary.com; © Giovanni Simeone/SIME-
4Corners Images.

The paper used for this book has been independently certified as having
been sourced from well-managed forests and recycled wood or fibre
according to the rules of the Forest Stewardship Council.
This book has been printed and bound in Italy by Printer Trento S.r.l.,
an FSC certified company for printing books on FSC mixed paper in
compliance with the chain of custody and on products labelling standards.

FSC
Mixed Sources
Product group from well-managed
forests and recycled wood or fibre
Cert no. CQ-COC-000012
www.fsc.org
© 1996 Forest Stewardship Council

Contents

Introduction

To understand Hawaii, you must understand 'aloha', *the most famous word in the Hawaiian language. Often rendered too simply as 'hello', 'goodbye' and 'love', 'aloha' actually means far more to the people of Hawaii, as a philosophy of treating each other and the natural world with affection, respect and genuine hospitality. Visitors to Hawaii soon learn that the spirit of* 'aloha' *is just as much a way of life as a state of mind.*

Indeed, the word 'hospitality' has become universally synonymous with Hawaii, and you'll see and feel it everywhere, from the colourful flower *lei* placed on your shoulders as greeting to the quiet strains of island music always floating in the background, from the friendly, helpful service offered at every shop and street corner to the beaming smiles of the *hula* dancers performing at a grand island feast.

But perhaps people are just naturally more friendly and relaxed when they live surrounded by the amazing natural beauty found everywhere in Hawaii. Certainly its superb settings are what

Diamond Head provides an ancient backdrop for the modern city of Honolulu

have made Hawaii one of the world's top travel destinations: the delightful white-sand beaches and cool upcountry pastures of Maui; the pristine mountain forests and soaring sea cliffs of Kauai; and the rough beauty and stark wonder of the lava flows and volcanic landscapes of Hawai`i the Big Island. Even Hawaii's oldest and most tourist-thronged holiday spot – the lively beach, bustling streets and gleaming high-rise hotels of Oahu's Waikiki – has a picturesque ocean view rounded out by the quietly grand beauty of Diamond Head, a 200,000-year-old volcanic crater.

Its eminence as one of the world's favourite summer playgrounds means Hawaii has a nearly infinite range of accommodations, restaurants, shops and activities designed to please, with top-notch locations for devotees of surfing, golfing, diving and hiking – or even for those who simply want to lie in a hammock and listen to the waves pounding the beach. And yet for all its modern tourist development, much of Hawaii still feels quietly rural and largely untouched, with great areas of beautiful wilderness to explore well away from the crowds.

Besides its natural beauty, many love Hawaii for its fascinating and diverse cultural history as well. Although the Polynesian origins of the native Hawaiian culture stand at the fore, 200 years of migration to Hawaii have made it one of the most ethnically diverse and culturally tolerant societies

An alluring beach on Kauai's north shore

in the world, and the heritage and traditions of Hawaii's many migrant groups – Chinese, Japanese, Portuguese, Filipino, Korean and more – have mixed with the dominant American lifestyle to make a unique island culture all its own. The spirit of *aloha*, after all, is all about acceptance and harmony, and no matter what their point of origin, residents of Hawaii are known as *kama`aina*, or 'children of the land'.

So don't be surprised if you find yourself dreaming of Hawaii long after you leave, or even returning again and again for future visits, as millions of visitors do every year. If you find yourself longing for the palm-lined beaches, the warm sea breezes and the kind smiles, you'll finally understand what *aloha* is all about.

The islands

The tropical islands of Hawaii are the most remote population centres in the world, sitting in splendid isolation halfway across the Pacific Ocean, with the nearest major landmass of North America about 2,300 miles (3,700km) away. Once barren mounds of lava formed by undersea volcanoes, they now hold a fascinatingly diverse ecology of flora and fauna, all of which either got there by accident – a floating seed, or a migrating bird blown off course – or were intentionally introduced and cultivated by human settlers.

The islands and atolls of the entire Hawaiian archipelago extend for 1,500 miles (2,400km) across the ocean, although only the eight most southeastern islands, occupying a total of 10,931sq miles (29,311sq km), were ever inhabited. Of these, six are open to

Tropical flowers like heliconias abound throughout the islands

tourism: the 'main four' of Oahu, Maui, Hawai`i (called the Big Island to avoid confusion) and Kauai, as well as the smaller, less-visited islands of Molokai and Lanai. The remaining two, Ni`ihau and Kaho`olawe, are off limits to visitors (*see p108*).

Hawaii was made the 50th state of the USA in 1959. Its capital Honolulu, located on the island of Oahu, is the home of the majority of the 1.2 million residents and sees the highest proportion of out-of-state visitors as well, due largely to its famous beach resort Waikiki. Other significant population centres are found at Lahaina and Kahului on Maui, Kailua and Hilo on Hawai`i the Big Island, and around Lihu`e and Kapa`a on Kauai.

Due to a variety of factors, the islands each have differing ecologies, but they do share a number of general similarities. All have central mountains which formed from one or more volcanoes, with settlements generally

The islands

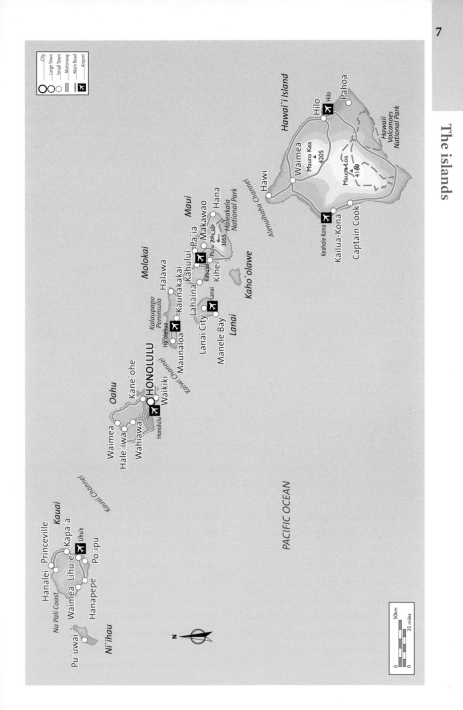

Key:
○ City
○ Large Town
○ Small Town
Motorway
Main Road
✈ Airport

N

Ni'ihau
Pu'uwai

Kauai
Hanalei Princeville
Na Pali Coast Kapa'a
Waimea Lihu'e ✈ Lihue
Hanapepe Po'ipu

Kauai Channel

PACIFIC OCEAN

Oahu
Waimea
Hale'iwa
Wahiawa Kane'ohe
HONOLULU ✈
Waikiki
Honolulu

Kaiwi Channel

Molokai
Kalaupapa
Peninsula
Ho'olehua ✈
Maunaloa Kaunakakai Halawa

Lanai
Lanai City
Lanai ✈
Manele Bay

Kaho'olawe

Maui
Kahului ✈ Pa'ia Makawao
Lahaina Pu'u 'Ula'ula
Kihei 3055 Hana
Haleakala
National Park

Alenuihaha Channel

Hawai'i Island
Hawi
Waimea Hilo ✈ Hilo
Mauna Kea
▲ 4205
Keahole Kona ✈ Mauna Loa
Kailua-Kona ▲ 4169
Captain Cook Hawaii
Volcanoes
National Park
Pahoa

0 ___ 50km
0 ___ 25 miles

The Na Pali cliffs on Kauai start beyond Ke`e Beach

ringing the coastal lowlands or dotting the lower montane regions. The position of the islands with regard to the Pacific trade winds gives them 'windward' sides to the north and east and 'leeward' sides to the south and west. The windward sides are often slightly cooler and more green and lush from the trade winds' rains, while the leeward sides – blocked from the winds by the central mountain ridges – are usually a bit hotter and drier (and thus where you'll find many of Hawaii's beach resorts). Beyond that, there's an amazing array of small climatic zones to be found all over Hawaii, from grassy plains and volcanic deserts to tropical rainforests and even the snow-peaked alpine region of the Big Island's Mauna Kea, which at 13,796ft (4,205m) is the highest mountain in the entire Pacific.

Hawaii abounds in vegetation of all sorts, of which about 89 per cent is found nowhere else on earth. Tropical flowers like bougainvillea, hibiscus and frangipani are common, as are trees like coconut palms, *koa* and `*ohi*`*a lehua*. In isolation from predators, flora evolved without the defence mechanisms normally found in mainland cousins, such as the thornless `*akala*, a native Hawaiian raspberry. The most singular endemic plant is the `*ahinahina*, better known by its English name, the Hawaiian silversword. One of a small subspecies of sunflower, it grows only in the volcanic cinder of the alpine desert atop Maui's massive mountain Haleakala, at elevations between 7,000 and 10,000ft (2,100–3,000m) above sea level.

Hawaii's native wildlife consists mostly of insects, birds and marine life; all of its land animals, mainly pigs, dogs,

HAWAIIAN PLACE NAMES

Although the `*okina* mark (*see p156*) is accurately found in the names of every island except Maui – that is, O`ahu, Kaua`i, Hawai`i, Moloka`i, Lana`i, Ni`ihau and Kaho`olawe – you'll rarely see them used in conventional English spellings, and the official name of the US state is simply 'Hawaii'.

This book uses *okinas* in the following cases: for the island of Hawai`i (usually called the Big Island), to distinguish it from Hawaii the state or former kingdom; for place and proper names on the islands themselves; and for the islands of Ni`ihau and Kaho`olawe, since they are still considered sites of traditional and cultural importance to native Hawaiians.

goats, horses and cows, were brought over either by its earliest Polynesian settlers or by later migrations of Americans, Europeans and Asians (as was, accidentally, the mosquito, which hatched from larvae in stale water emptied out by a whaling ship in the early 1800s). The state bird is the *nene*, or Hawaiian goose, but other birds include several dozen subspecies of honeycreepers, all descended from one small flock of cardueline finches believed to have landed on the islands three to four million years ago. Marine wildlife includes numerous tropical fishes found on the islands' offshore reefs, monk seals, green sea turtles, spinner dolphins and the Pacific humpback whale, whose yearly migrations offer visitors the chance to see them frolicking in Hawaii's shallow coastal waters, particularly between Maui and Lanai.

The state bird is the nene, a flightless goose

The islands

Volcanoes

Central to life in Hawaii – both figuratively and literally – are the massive volcanoes that created the islands, perpetuating an endless cycle of creation and destruction through their lava flows. This lava formed the islands, eventually breaking down into the rich, volcanic soil responsible for Hawaii's lush flora, and even today is re-forming them, with several square miles of new coastline added to Hawai`i the Big Island since 1983 thanks to the continuous eruption of Kilauea.

The Hawaiian islands are the youngest links in a chain of dozens of undersea volcanoes stretching 3,500 miles (5,600km) to the northwest. Over the past 70 million years, each volcano has grown in succession as the Pacific plate moves slowly over a stationary 'hot spot' (or mantle plume) spewing magma up from the earth's core and through the ocean floor. These plate movements caused multiple volcanoes to form in close proximity on each island, as with the 'doublet' of Maui's two volcanic ridges, or the five individual volcanoes that make up the Big Island. Unlike the pointy-topped 'composite' volcanoes of popular imagination, Hawaii's 'shield' volcanoes have a rounded, gently sloping shape created

Pahoehoe lava on Hawai`i the Big Island

Rough a`a lava from the last flows on Maui in 1790

slowly and steadily by layer upon layer of fluid lava seeping out of rifts and eventually drying.

Various factors like temperature, viscosity and location create different types of lava flow, known by their Hawaiian names: *a`a* for rough, broken lava and *pahoehoe* for the smoother, more billowy kind. Other by-products include glassy filaments called 'Pele's hair' and droplets called 'Pele's tears', both named after the Hawaiian volcano goddess (*see text box*). Smaller cones and craters also formed from vents along the mountains' flanks, creating the long-extinct Diamond Head (Oahu) and Molokini Crater (Maui) as well as active ones like Kilauea's spatter cone

Pu`u `O`o. Over time, as each island moved off the hot spot, their volcanoes went extinct, and erosion from wind and water further whittled them to their present shapes – the sheer sea cliffs of Molokai and Kauai, for example, were formed by landslides when parts of their eroded volcanoes collapsed into the sea.

Ni`ihau and Kauai, the oldest Hawaiian islands, were formed about five million years ago, while the Big Island was born less than half a million years ago, and is still growing today. The newest addition to the chain is a seamount (submerged volcano) called Lo`ihi, which lies 19 miles (30km) south of the Big Island, about half a mile (1km) below sea level. If its eruptions continue at constant rates, it's expected to emerge from the ocean in the next 50,000 years or so.

THE VOLCANO GODDESS

Pele, the Hawaiian goddess of volcanoes and fire, was exiled from her home in Tahiti because of her violent temper and difficult personality. Chased by an angry older sister, Pele fled to the Hawaiian islands, creating volcanoes as she landed – first on Kauai and then southeast across the others, until her sister finally gave up and Pele could make her home in the Big Island's Kilauea Crater, where she lives today. She's said to appear to humans as an old woman asking for help or food, rewarding those who treat her kindly and punishing the disrespectful.

History

CE **300–600**	Polynesians from the Marquesas Islands sail 3,000 miles (5,000km) across the Pacific Ocean, beginning new colonies on Hawaiian islands.
1000–1300	More Polynesians from the Society Islands (Tahiti) invade, introducing a strict class system and the laws of *kapu* (taboo).
1758	Kamehameha the Great is born on Hawai`i (the Big Island).
1778	English captain James Cook lands at Waimea, Kauai. He names the archipelago 'The Sandwich Islands'.
1779	Cook killed by Hawaiians at Kealakekua Bay, Hawai`i.
1791–5	Kamehameha vanquishes rival chiefs.
1810	Chief of Kauai cedes power. King Kamehameha I rules the first united Kingdom of Hawai`i.
1819	Kamehameha I dies; his son becomes Kamehameha II.
1820	First missionaries arrive at Kailua Bay, Hawai`i.
1824	Kamehameha II dies. His 11-year-old brother becomes Kamehameha III under the Queen Regent.
1832	First sugar plantations founded on Kauai. Queen Ka`ahumanu dies. All of Hawaii now Christian.
1840	Kamehameha III creates Hawaii's first constitution.
1848	Kamehameha III announces the Great *Mahele* ('land division'). Millions of acres of land released for sale; white plantation owners purchase most of it.
1852	First foreign contract labourers imported for plantation work from China, followed in later years by Japanese, Koreans, Portuguese and others.
1853	Smallpox epidemic kills several thousands.
1854	Kamehameha III dies; his nephew becomes Kamehameha IV.

1863	Kamehameha IV dies; his brother becomes Kamehameha V.
1872	Kamehameha V dies without naming a successor. Monarchs now decided by popular vote.
1873	William Lunalilo, cousin of Kamehameha V, becomes first elected king, but dies after only a year of rule.
1874	King David Kalakaua is elected to the crown.
1876	The Treaty of Reciprocity abolishes trade tariffs between the US and the Kingdom of Hawaii.
1887	White business owners force Kalakaua to approve the 'Bayonet Constitution', giving property holders power over the legislature.
1889	Father Damien, caretaker of Kalaupapa, dies.
1891	Kalakaua dies while abroad in San Francisco; his sister becomes queen.
1893	Queen Lili`uokalani deposed by white businessmen. Sanford Dole forms provisional government for the Republic of Hawaii.
1895	Royalist coup fails. Lili`uokalani charged with treason.
1898	Hawaii annexed as a US territory by President William McKinley. Sanford Dole appointed governor.
1936	First commercial flights to Hawaii; tourist trade grows.
1941	Japanese planes attack Pearl Harbor; US enters World War II.
1946–7	Newly unionised workers gain first victories from strikes at sugar and pineapple plantations.
1959	Hawaii becomes 50th US state.
1986	John Waihe`e becomes first native-Hawaiian governor.
1995	Last sugar plantation on island of Hawai`i closes.
2002	Linda Lingle becomes first female governor.
2007	Disney announces plans to open a resort on Oahu.

Politics

Hawaii's modern political history has been brief but volatile, having experienced feudal tribalism, unified monarchy, territorial oligarchy and full American statehood all in just under 200 years. Along the way, the native Hawaiian population has been complemented – and, sadly, decimated – by numerous groups from abroad, ranging from Western missionaries and business owners to Eastern farm workers. The resulting cultural mélange is today one of the world's most ethnically diverse societies.

Administration

The 50th US state, Hawaii has a state government of three branches, historically dominated by the Democratic Party: an executive (at the time of writing, Governor Linda Lingle, one of the few Republicans), a bicameral legislature and a state judiciary, all located in Honolulu, the capital and only incorporated city in Hawaii. Hawaii has four representatives in the federal legislature: two in the Senate and two in the House of Representatives. Hawaii has four municipal governments: the County of Hawaii (the Big Island), the County of Kauai (includes Ni`ihau), the County of Maui (includes Molokai, Lanai and Kaho`olawe) and the City and County of Honolulu, which covers the entire island of Oahu.

Modern political history

After annexation by the US in 1898, Hawaii continued to be controlled by the directors of the 'Big Five', the top agribusiness companies who dominated government and all other industries. They had no interest in statehood, preferring to keep the population of native Hawaiians and immigrants disenfranchised. In the late 1930s, American union leaders tried to organise workers, to little avail. Once Pearl Harbor was attacked in 1941, however, the US government declared martial law and took control for the next five years. After the war, a new generation of labour activists – who, being born in a US territory, could claim American citizenship and protection under its labour laws – had their first victory, a general strike that shut down the plantations for several months. This and other efforts brought about sweeping political and social changes that broke the control of the Big Five and led, ultimately, to the closing of the plantations. In 1959, the US government offered statehood and the people of Hawaii voted 17-to-1 in favour. Since then, the industries of tourism and real estate have flourished in the vacuum left behind by the loss of the sugar-and-pineapple economy.

Current issues

The most contentious issue in Hawaii today is restoration of Hawaiian sovereignty, which first gained support in the late 1980s and early '90s with the campaign for the island of Kaho`olawe (*see p108*). In 1993, after mass demonstrations commemorating the centennial of the overthrow of Queen Lili`uokalani, President Clinton signed an official apology acknowledging the illegality of the coup. This was thought by many to be a promising first step, but opinions within the state were greatly divided, with some wanting Hawaii to be a fully independent nation again, others wanting 'nation within a nation' status for native Hawaiians, and a large group wanting to stay in the US but have economic reparations made to native Hawaiians. Although the state government is generally sympathetic to Hawaiian causes, the current Republican administration in Washington has shown no interest in further investigating any form of Hawaiian sovereignty.

Politics

The issue of restoring Hawaiian sovereignty has not yet been resolved

The Hawaiian monarchy

The sovereign Kingdom of Hawaii lasted for nearly a century, from its founding in 1795 until its overthrow in 1893. Its eight rulers came from two noble family dynasties: the House of Kamehameha and the House of Kalakaua.

King Kamehameha I (1795–1819)

A great warrior and chief from Kohala on the Big Island, Kamehameha set out in 1791 to bring all the islands under one rule, conquering all by 1795 except for Kauai and Ni`ihau, which finally joined the kingdom in 1810.

King Kamehameha II (1819–24)

Kamehameha's son Liholiho assumed the throne at age 22, with his stepmother Queen Ka`ahumanu as regent; she soon dismantled the ancient *kapu* laws by dining with him in public, an act formerly forbidden. Liholiho allowed Hawaii's first missionaries to reside in Kailua and Honolulu. He and his wife died of measles in London on a futile trip to meet King George IV.

King Kamehameha III (1825–54)

Liholiho's younger brother Kauikeaouli was 11 when he assumed the throne,

The royal crest of the Kingdom of Hawaii: 'The Life of the Land is Perpetuated in Righteousness'

with Ka`ahumanu still regent. Influenced by *haole* (non-Hawaiian) advisors, his Great Mahele ('land division') of 1848 introduced private land ownership, leading to foreigners buying up most of the land.

King Kamehameha IV (1855–63)

Alexander Liholiho, grandson of Kamehameha I and nephew of Kamehameha III, attempted to fight the growing foreign influence in business and government and introduce better healthcare for Hawaiians (who were dying from imported diseases at alarming rates), but could do little before his untimely death.

King Kamehameha V (1863–72)

Lot Kapuaiwa, younger brother to Kamehameha IV, was the dynasty's last king. He banished Hawaiians with leprosy to the island of Molokai and introduced a new constitution strengthening the power of the monarchy. He died without naming an heir, forcing the legislature to call an open election for the throne.

King William Lunalilo (1873–4)

A cousin to Kamehameha V, Lunalilo was tremendously popular and beat rival chief David Kalakaua by a landslide. He planned to repair Hawaii's flagging economy and re-democratise the government by amending the previous constitution, but died after only a year, forcing another election, this time won by Kalakaua.

King David Kalakaua (1874–91)

Known for his love of the good life, the 'Merrie Monarch' revived traditional Hawaiian culture like *hula* and surfing but was forced by Hawaii's white business élite to eliminate tariffs on agricultural exports to the US and sign the 'Bayonet Constitution' removing most of the king's executive power and shifting voting rights in favour of non-Hawaiians. He died childless, naming his sister as heir.

Queen Lili`uokalani (1891–3)

Lili`uokalani soon announced her intention to replace the previous constitution and restore power to the crown. A committee led by white businessmen Lorrin Thurston and Sanford Dole (both from missionary families) deposed the queen in 1893. Dole became the first president of the Republic of Hawaii in 1894, formalising the end of the monarchy. Lili`uokalani spent a year under house arrest in `Iolani Palace, retiring to Washington Place afterwards, and died in 1917 at the age of 79.

Culture

Much of Hawaiian culture was almost stamped out by the early Christian missionaries, who tried to repress such 'heathen' aspects of their new converts. In the late 19th century, King David Kalakaua encouraged a great revival of traditional Hawaiian music and dance – the popular, annual Merrie Monarch Festival is named after him – and since then, Hawaiian heritage has made a strong comeback and become a source of great cultural pride across the islands.

Crafts

Before contact from the wider world, indigenous Hawaiians had no workable clays or metals in their soil, so all of their utensils and objects for daily life had to be made from natural materials at hand, such as plants, trees, animals and stone. Hollowed-out fruit shells were used as vessels for drinking water, while bowls and eating utensils were carved from wood. Stone implements were shaped for pounding the roots of the taro plant to make *poi*, a thick paste that was a staple of the Hawaiian diet. Thin, strong fibres from the *olona* shrub were used to make fishing nets, or for use as fasteners. Oil from the *kukui* nut (also known as the

Carrying on the tradition of weaving from palm leaves

Ancient Hawaiians ate from wooden bowls like these

candlenut) was extracted and burnt for light in stone lamps or in torches made from *ti* leaves. Canoes were hollowed out from the trunks of *koa* trees (a type of Acacia), whose prized dark-red wood is also seen in furniture and musical instruments. Other furnishings, surfboards and fish-net floats were made from the lightweight wood of *ulu* (breadfruit) and *wiliwili* (coral tree). Rounded boulders from river beds and volcanic lava rocks were hauled and stacked to make platforms for *heiaus* (temples) and walls for fish-ponds (*see p114*).

Cloth for most garments was made from *kapa*, or pounded bark. The best *kapa* cloth was made from the *wauke* (paper mulberry) tree, decorated with plant-based dyes and stamped with patterns using bamboo. Other objects, like baskets, fans and sleeping mats,

were tightly woven or plaited from various leaves and grass, including the *hala* (pandanus) tree, coconut palms and *makaloa* (sedge grass). Ceremonial clothing for the *ali`i* (chiefs and nobles), like capes and headdresses, were painstakingly made in bright colours using thousands of bird feathers from native species of finches – red from the `i`iwi (scarlet Hawaiian honeycreeper) and yellow from the `o`o (Hawaiian mamo), now extinct. Perhaps the most famous Hawaiian handicrafts are the beautiful *leis* made from flowers, shells, feathers and *kukui* nuts and worn as garlands around the neck. These are still made all over the islands, especially for Lei Day celebrations in May, and are popular souvenirs for visitors.

Dance and music

Universally synonymous with Hawaii is *hula*, a form of dance used for both sacred religious ritual and as entertainment for the ruling classes. The traditional form, *hula kahiko*, was performed to percussion instruments and vocalists singing *mele*, the chanted songs that recounted tales, poetry and *ali`i* bloodlines from thousands of years of Hawaiian oral history. Male and female *hula* dancers wore skirts of long, flat *ti* leaves or *kapa* cloth, and anklets or bracelets made from fern leaves. Men also wore leg ornaments made from dogs' teeth, known as *kupe`e niho `ilio*, which rattled in time with their movements. Percussion instruments used by the dancers included *pu`ili* (split bamboo sticks) and *`uli`uli* (seed-filled gourds decorated with feathers), while accompanists played the *ipu heke* (double-gourd drum) and the *pahu* and *puniu*, large and small drums made from trees and coconuts and covered with stretched shark or fish skin.

When *hula* dancing saw its resurgence during King Kalakaua's time, new elements were incorporated into it, leading to the modern style known as *hula `auwana*. Dancers now wore more 'modest' clothing like long-sleeved, full-length dresses, as well as flower *leis*, and were accompanied by imported instruments that soon became staples of Hawaiian music: the *ukelele* ('jumping flea'), a small,

four-stringed guitar that originated with Portuguese migrants; a six-string guitar – often used with an open tuning known as 'slack key', or played horizontally with a metal rod used for glissando effects, known as 'steel guitar'; and a standing bass.

Many *hula* dances seen today, especially at tourist *lu`aus*, use a mix of styles from both the *kahiko* and *`auwana* schools. In recent decades, Hawaiian music has also developed new styles and forms from the many foreign influences brought to the islands by various ethnic groups, including *hapa haole* (English lyrics set to Hawaiian melodies) and a mix of Hawaiian and Jamaican reggae music known as Jawaiian.

Oral and literary tradition

Ancient Hawaii's oral tradition was composed, recited and passed on by the *kahuna* (priests) in the form of the *mele* chants and songs. The principal creation belief, the *Kumulipo*, recounts – unusually, with no creator god – how the earth and all its creatures developed over ages and ages, from 'slime' in the darkness to more complex life forms like coral, pigs and finally humans. After a hundred generations, the humans progressed into divine beings, and the ancestors of the Hawaiian people were born: *Wakea*, god of the heavens, and *Papa*, goddess of the earth, whose children were the taro plant (sacred sustenance for Hawaiians), the first Hawaiian humans

The *ukelele* is universally associated with Hawaiian music

and the islands themselves – although in other stories, the islands were created by the demigod Maui (*see p100*).

Although Hawaiians had no written tradition, a number of well-known Western writers, captivated by their travels around the islands, wrote about Hawaii or used their experiences there as a basis for other works. Herman Melville spent four months in Honolulu and Lahaina in 1843 during a long voyage around the South Pacific, which later inspired his famous novels *Typee*, *Omoo* and *Moby Dick*. In 1866, a young Mark Twain was commissioned by a California newspaper to write about Hawaii in *Letters from the Sandwich Islands*

(later reworked in his book *Roughing It*), in which he described the spectacular scene of an erupting volcano on the Big Island. Robert Louis Stevenson, suffering from tuberculosis, moved to the South Pacific and spent half a year in Hawaii, where he befriended both King David Kalakaua and his niece, Princess Victoria, and wrote *The Master of Ballantrae* and the stories 'The Isle of Voices' and 'The Bottle Imp'. In the early 20th century, Jack London visited Hawaii often, writing *The Call of the Wild* and *White Fang* there, as well as two volumes of stories set in the islands, including his biographical tale, 'Ko`olau the Leper' (*see p123*).

A *hula* dancer wears a skirt of *ti* leaves and plays a gourd percussion instrument

Festivals and events

Thanks to temperate weather, wondrous natural settings, a multicultural mix of world heritages and a steady stream of fun-seeking visitors, Hawaii sees a more or less constant parade of festivals and events year-round. Some, like various athletic competitions, bring together experts from around the globe, while others are the artistic and cultural expressions of dedicated locals. Whether you prefer to be a spectator or a participant, you'll rarely be far from some local event that will pique your interest.

With festivals occurring both state-wide and on specific islands, there are far more than can be listed here. Be sure to check online, with local tourist boards or your hotel for events that coincide with your holiday plans, especially since many of the larger ones require advance booking for tickets or accommodation.

January
Maui Pro Surf Meet (Maui)
Hula Bowl (Maui) – US college football (gridiron) tournament
Ka Molokai Makahiki (Molokai) – Hawaiian cultural festival

Hilo's Merrie Monarch Festival was named after King David Kalakaua, who spurred a revival of traditional Hawaiian culture

Narcissus Festival (Oahu, Jan–Feb) – Chinese cultural festival

February
Cherry Blossom Festival (Oahu, Feb–Mar) – Japanese cultural festival
Hilo Mardi Gras (Big Island)
Great Maui Whale Festival (Maui)
NFL Pro Bowl (Honolulu, Oahu) – post-season professional football (gridiron) game

March
St Patrick's Day Parade (Waikiki, Oahu, 17 March)
Prince Kuhio Day (state holiday, 26 March)
Windward Orchid Society Annual Spring Show (Oahu)

April
Easter Sunrise Service (Punchbowl Crater, Oahu)
Merrie Monarch Festival (Hilo, Big Island) – very popular cultural festival and *hula* competition

May
Lei Day (state holiday, 1 May) – *lei*-making demonstrations and contests
Molokai Ka Hula Piko (Molokai, 3rd Sat) – *hula* dance festival
International Festival of Canoes (Maui)

June
King Kamehameha Day (state holiday, 11 June) – parades, performances and craft fairs
Kiho`alu Hawaiian Slack-Key Guitar Festival (Maui)
O-Bon Festival (all islands, June–Aug) – Japanese Buddhist festival and dances

July
Makawao Rodeo (Maui, 4 July)
Parker Ranch Rodeo (Big Island, 4 July)
Hawaii International Jazz Festival (Honolulu, Oahu)
Koloa Plantation Days (Kauai) – celebration of Hawaiian sugar-cane industry
Pu`uhonua O Honaunau Cultural Festival (Big Island) – Hawaiian historical festival and royal court re-creation
Quicksilver Cup Windsurfing Competition (Maui)

August
Hawaiian International Billfish Tournament (Big Island) – big-game fishing invitational

September
Aloha Week (all islands, Sept–Oct) – Hawaii's largest arts and cultural festival, held for one week on each island
A Taste of Lahaina (Maui) – culinary and tasting festival

October
Halloween Parade (Lahaina, Maui & Waikiki, Oahu, 31 Oct)
Aloha Classic Windsurfing Championships (Maui, Oct–Nov)
Hamakua Music Festival (Big Island)
Ironman Triathlon World Championship (Big Island)
Na Molokai Hoe (Molokai) – outrigger canoe race to Oahu

November
Hawaii International Film Festival (Oahu, other islands)
Kona Coffee Cultural Festival (Big Island)
Mission Houses Museum Holiday Crafts Fair (Honolulu, Oahu)
Triple Crown of Surfing World Cup (Oahu, Nov–Dec)
World Invitation Hula Festival (Honolulu, Oahu)

December
Hawaii Bowl (Honolulu, Oahu, 25 Dec) – US college football (gridiron) tournament
Honolulu Marathon (Oahu, 2nd Sun)
PGA Grand Slam (Kauai) – championship golf tournament
Honolulu City Lights (Oahu)– Christmas-tree lighting festival
Na Mele O Maui (Ka`anapali, Maui) – Hawaiian cultural and music festival

Highlights

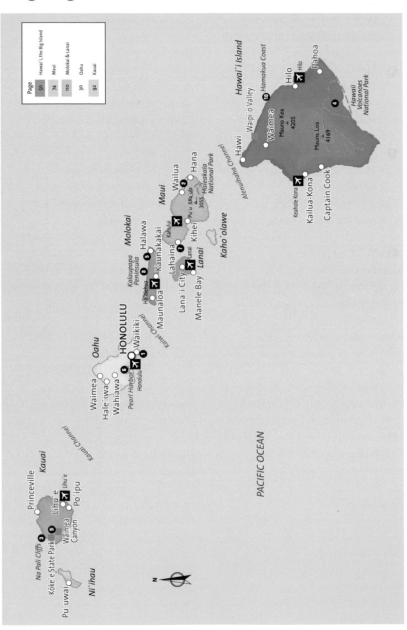

Page	
50	Hawai'i, the Big Island
74	Maui
110	Molokai & Lanai
30	Oahu
92	Kauai

❶ Waikiki Beach, Oahu
Hawaii's most famous and most lively beach is great for surfing, sun-bathing and people-watching.

❷ The Hana Highway, Maui
Steep, twisting roads and waterfall-dotted valleys make this one of the world's most scenic drives.

❸ Na Pali cliffs, Kauai
Take a helicopter tour over these stunning seacliffs and the otherwise inaccessible mountain ridges of the Garden Isle.

❹ Volcanoes National Park, Hawai`i the Big Island
Marvel at the power of nature at one of the active volcanoes that helped form this island chain.

❺ Halawa Valley, Molokai
Step back in time in this lush, remote valley that was home to some of Hawaii's earliest settlers.

❻ USS *Arizona*, Pearl Harbor, Oahu
Pay tribute to the past at the military memorials that mark America's entry into World War II.

❼ Lahaina, Maui
Stroll through this harbour town steeped in history and watch humpback whales breaching just offshore.

❽ Kalaupapa Peninsula, Molokai
Ride a mule down to a former colony of exiles, once isolated beneath the highest seacliffs in the world.

❾ Waimea Canyon and Koke`e State Park, Kauai
Driving or hiking through the remote interior of Kauai offers spectacular views of Hawaii's 'Grand Canyon of the Pacific'.

❿ Hamakua Coast, Hawai`i the Big Island
Explore the Big Island's windward coast, from the grandeur of Waipi`o Valley and `Akaka Falls to the vintage charm of Hilo town.

The Hana Highway, Maui

Suggested itineraries

With six islands full of things to see, a trip to Hawaii can be challenging to plan. Unless you're lucky enough to have several months to tour the archipelago, you'll probably only have time to either make brief visits to a few islands or enjoy a more comprehensive trip on just one or two of them. The first step is figuring out what kind of trip you want – beach fun, mountain hiking, nightlife or shops – and then choosing the island(s) that best suit your needs.

It's not difficult to fit in more than one island, thanks to the many daily inter-island flights, although be sure to coordinate which airport you want to fly into or out of (most of the islands have more than one), and keep in mind that many, though not all, inter-island routes have to go through Honolulu first. Although the hops are short, often only around 30–45 minutes each, with travel to and from airports plus hotel and hire-car check-ins and -outs, assume that any inter-island flight will take up half a day's travelling time. Take early flights for better prices and more time to spend at your next destination.

ISLAND-WIDE
Long weekend

Most international flights fly into Oahu, where Waikiki is a great destination for a few days. Otherwise, catch a connecting flight to another island and pick one area there to stay.

One week

A week is enough time to explore any one island quite well, or else spend a few days seeing the highlights on two of the main four islands (Oahu, Maui, Kauai or Hawai`i the Big Island).

Two weeks

Pick two islands and spend a relaxing week on each of them, perhaps even taking two days on Molokai or a day trip to Lanai. If you want to get more in, take shorter jaunts around the highlights of your favourite three islands – but you'll want to allow at least a week for the Big Island, if not more.

Longer

Depending on your time frame, you can spend a few days or a week each on all four main islands, and take a side trip to Molokai and/or Lanai. For most visitors, there's little reason to spend more than two weeks on any one island, unless your main goal is just relaxing on a tropical beach and taking the occasional leisurely day trip or hike without a lot of inter-island travelling.

OAHU
Long weekend

Spend the weekend in Waikiki, with half-day trips to downtown Honolulu or Pearl Harbor. Spend a day snorkelling at Hanauma Bay or driving around the southeast.

One week

Enjoy bustling Waikiki and take a few day trips around Greater Honolulu and the southeast. Or move to the North Shore after a few days to further explore the surrounding coastline and relax away from Waikiki.

Two weeks

If you get bored of Waikiki after a few days, try moving to southeast Oahu and/or the North Shore for some more relaxing beach time without the crowds.

HAWAI`I, THE BIG ISLAND
Long weekend

Relax on the beaches of Kohala or the Kona Coast, or stay in Hilo or the southeast to fully explore Volcanoes National Park.

One week

Spend a week in Kailua-Kona, with day trips along the coast and through Kohala, or stay in Hilo to have more time at the volcanoes, Puna and the Hamakua Coast. Alternatively, spend a few days in northern Kohala to explore upcountry and the Hamakua Coast, with a day trip up Mauna Kea, and then a few days in either Hilo or Kailua-Kona.

Two weeks

Spend a few days in Hilo and explore the southeast and the volcanoes, move up the Hamakua Coast and spend a few days in upcountry Kohala or Waimea, and then laze on a beach for a week in southern Kohala or Kailua-Kona.

Suggested itineraries

The beach at Turtle Bay on Oahu's north shore

The drive to East Maui offers stunning coastal scenery

MAUI
Long weekend
Stay on the leeward coast and enjoy its beaches and snorkelling at Molokini Crater. Take a day trip to see Lahaina, `Iao Valley and the north coast, or an upcountry drive to the summit of Haleakala.

One week
Base yourself in Lahaina, the leeward coast or the north shore, and take day trips to everywhere else, or split a few days each between upcountry and the beaches. Drive the road to Hana, perhaps staying there overnight for a more relaxing return drive.

Two weeks
You can split your time between two contrasting areas, such as beaches and upcountry, and have time to leisurely explore the rest. Get up early one morning to catch a breathtaking sunrise over the crater at Haleakala. Drive to Hana and spend a few days relaxing at Hamoa Beach and exploring the east coast. Take a day trip to Lanai or Molokai.

KAUAI
Long weekend
Base yourself up north near Hanalei or down south in Po`ipu to relax on the beach. From the north take a day trip

around the coast. In the south, drive up to the Waimea Canyon lookouts. Take a short helicopter trip over the island from either coast.

One week

Stay on the east coast around Kapa`a, and take leisurely day trips around the island in both directions. Take a boat trip with a sunset dinner to the Na Pali Coast, or a helicopter trip around the island from Lihu`e. Or relax a little longer in a resort at Hanalei or Po`ipu.

Two weeks

Spend a week relaxing at each end of the island. Take a full day to do a hike in Koke`e State Park or to Hanakapi`ai Valley. If you don't mind the expense, take a day trip to snorkel the untouched beaches of neighbouring Ni`ihau.

MOLOKAI AND LANAI
Long weekend

Hole up at a plush resort on Lanai, or relax on laid-back Molokai, with a day trip to the Kalaupapa Peninsula or Halawa Valley.

One week

Spend a week on Molokai, with day trips to both Kalaupapa and Halawa, and even one to Lanai. Or spend your time fully exploring Lanai, with a day cruise to Lahaina, Maui.

Two weeks

Spend a week each on Molokai and Lanai, or else split the time up between them and Maui.

Suggested itineraries

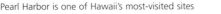

Pearl Harbor is one of Hawaii's most-visited sites

Honolulu and Oahu

Oahu's nickname is 'The Gathering Place', and it's apt; approximately 75 per cent of Hawaii's population, around 900,000 people, live here, with about half of those in Honolulu, the state capital and economic centre of the entire archipelago. It's also the centre of the tourism industry, thanks to its large international airport and the beach area of Waikiki, home to nearly all the hotel rooms on the island and where nine out of ten visitors spend at least one night of their trip.

Oahu has the largest number of tourist attractions and activities in the islands, and yet many consider it the 'least Hawaiian' to visit. Waikiki can be exciting but it also has a generic beach-resort atmosphere, so if you're after anything more rustic or cultural, plan day trips to other parts of the island.

Active sightseers can consider purchasing the **Go Oahu Card** (*www.gooahucard.com*), good for one to seven days, which offers free admission to many museums, cultural sights, tours and equipment hire, as well as some dining and shopping discounts.

Orientation

The third largest of the islands at 600sq miles (1,500sq km), Oahu consists of two blocks of volcanic mountains – the Wai`anae Range in the west and the longer, curving Ko`olau Range in the northeast – and the central plains in between. Pearl Harbor, Honolulu and Waikiki range along the leeward side of the southeastern tail, with the towns of Kane`ohe and Kailua across the mountains on the windward side, and the North Shore up on the northeast coast. The arid leeward coast has a number of rural towns and beaches but no tourist attractions.

Interstate highways H1, H2 and H3 radiate out from the Honolulu area. Some state highways you may encounter are the Nimitz Highway (92) that becomes the Ala Moana Boulevard,

The sands at Waikiki, Hawaii's most famous beach

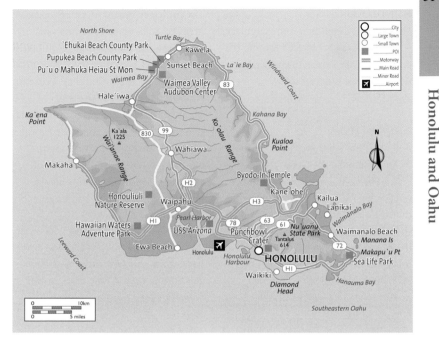

North Shore
'Ehukai Beach County Park
Pupukea Beach County Park
Pu'u o Mahuka Heiau St Mon
Turtle Bay
Kawela
Sunset Beach
La'ie Bay
Windward Coast
Waimea Bay
Waimea Valley
Audubon Center
83
Hale'iwa
Ka'ena Point
Kahana Bay
Ka'ala 1225
830
99
Ko'olau Range
Kualoa Point
Wahiawa
Wai'anae Range
Makaha
H2
Byodo-In Temple
Honouliuli Nature Reserve
Waipahu
Kane'ohe
H3
Kailua
Lanikai
Pearl Harbor
H1
78
63
61
Waimanalo Bay
Hawaiian Waters Adventure Park
USS Arizona
Punchbowl Crater
Nu'uanu State Park
Tantalus 614
Waimanalo Beach
Manana Is
Leeward Coast
'Ewa Beach
Honolulu
Honolulu Harbour
HONOLULU
72
Makapu'u Pt
Sea Life Park
Waikiki
H1
Diamond Head
Hanauma Bay
Southeastern Oahu

City
Large Town
Small Town
POI
Motorway
Main Road
Minor Road
Airport

0   10km
0   5 miles

the Pali Highway (61) and Likelike Highway (63) across the mountains to Kane'ohe Bay, the Kalanianaole Highway (72) that runs around the southeastern tip, and the Kamehameha Highway (99 and 83) that runs through the plains, along the North Shore and down the windward coast to Kane'ohe Bay. One can easily drive in a loop around the Ko'olau Range in a day, although to have more time to enjoy the sights, we recommend using one day just for southeast Oahu and another for the North Shore. Unlike the other islands, Oahu is covered by a comprehensive, inexpensive and reliable bus system, called TheBus (*see pp128–9*). It's your best bet for travel around Honolulu and Waikiki.

History

In ancient times Oahu was the least important of the four major islands. Kamehameha the Great conquered Oahu in 1795 (*see p49*) in his quest to unite the islands, and set up residence at Waikiki. By the early 19th century, Honolulu had become a thriving port for whaling ships, and by 1830 had a population of 10,000. American missionaries and business interests soon moved in, and King Kamehameha III transferred his capital back to Honolulu from Maui, ensuring its future. After the US annexation, Pearl Harbor became first a supply depot and then a major naval base, and the military presence on the island is still strong today.

HONOLULU

Downtown Honolulu is quite compact, with its main sights located around the graceful `Iolani Palace, the only royal residence on American soil.
Bus: 2, 13, B.

Ali`iolani Hale

A gold-painted and garlanded **statue of Kamehameha the Great**, the first king to rule a unified Hawaii, stands outside the Ali`iolani Hale ('House of the Heavenly King'), just across South King Street from `Iolani Palace. Built in 1874 as an intended royal residence, it became instead Hawaii's first library and a national museum, and now houses Hawaii's Supreme Court.

The **Judiciary History Center** (*open: Mon–Fri 8am–4pm; free admission*) on the ground floor features exhibits on the history of Hawaiian law.

Hawaii State Art Museum

Three galleries in a 1920s Spanish-style government building comprise Hawaii's most recently opened art museum, offering a rotating list of exhibits of contemporary art in various media, including photographs, paintings, sculpture and handicrafts.
2nd fl, No 1 Capitol Building, 250 South Hotel St. Tel: (808) 586-0900. www.hawaii.gov/sfca. Open: Tue–Sat 10am–4pm. Closed: Sun, Mon, public holidays. Free admission.

Ali`iolani Hale and the statue of King Kamehameha I

`Iolani Palace

King David Kalakaua based the design for `Iolani ('Royal Hawk') on Victorian architecture and took up residence in 1882. Only 11 years later his sister Queen Lili`uokalani was deposed by American businessmen and the palace became the seat of the new territorial government. Guided and audio tours take you through the former state apartments and private quarters, while the basement galleries display exhibits of royal regalia and artefacts. A **statue of Queen Lili`uokalani** stands behind the palace, looking over at the unconventional **State Capitol** building across the street.

King St & Richards St. Tel: (808) 522-0832. www.iolanipalace.org. Open: Tue–Sat 9am–4.30pm. Closed: Sun, Mon, New Year, 4 July, Thanksgiving, Christmas. Admission charge.

`Iolani Palace, the only royal residence on US soil

957 Punchbowl St. Tel: (808) 522-1333. Open: 8.30am–4pm. Closed: public holidays.

Kawaiaha`o Church

Dating back to the earliest Christian missionaries, this 1842 edifice – built from huge slabs of coral taken from the offshore reef – is the fifth church on this site. In front is the Gothic mausoleum of King Lunalilo, Hawaii's first elected king. At the back is a small cemetery with the graves of members of the élite missionary families who later became powerful plantation owners, including Sanford B Dole, the first (and only) president of the short-lived Republic of Hawaii. Across South King Street is the municipal seat of government, **Honolulu Hale**.

Mission Houses Museum

Directly east of the Kawaiaha`o Church are several restored mission houses from the 1820s, home to several missionary families and site of their storehouse and the printing press that produced the first Bible in the Hawaiian tongue. Guided tours take you inside the houses, and exhibits at the visitor centre explain the history of the missions and their impact on the islands.

553 South King St. Tel: (808) 531-0481. www.missionhouses.org. Open: Tue–Sat 10am–4pm, guided tours at 11am & 2.45pm. Closed: Sun, Mon, public holidays. Admission charge.

The Aloha Tower was Honolulu's first tourist landmark

Lili`uokalani in the 1860s, back when she was Mrs. Lydia Dominis, the wife of the royal governor of Oahu and Maui under King Kamehameha V. After her release from house arrest, she returned to Washington Place to live as a private citizen until her death in 1917. The house has been preserved as a museum to Hawaii's last queen, and the splendid rooms are still used by the governor (who resides next door) for important state events.
S Beretania St & Richards St. Tel: (808) 586-0248. www.hawaii.gov/gov/washington_place. Open: tours Mon–Fri by appointment only. Free admission.

St Andrew's Cathedral

St Andrew's started out as an Anglican cathedral in 1867, built to honour the aspirations of King Kamehameha IV, who attempted to bring Anglicanism to the islands to stop the spread of the more Puritanical streak of Christianity being preached by American missionaries. When Hawaii became an American territory in 1898, the congregation became Episcopalian, the American equivalent of the Church of England. Today St Andrew's is the oldest Episcopal church in Hawaii.
229 Queen Emma Sq. Tel: (808) 524-2822. www.saintandrewscathedral.net. Open: 6.30am–6pm.

Washington Place

This dignified Colonial-style mansion (built 1847) was the home of Queen

Waterfront Honolulu

The waterfront features the landmark Aloha Tower and its open-air shops and restaurants, a maritime museum, a beautiful waterfront park and beach and the city's largest shopping centres.
Bus: 19, 20, 42.

Ala Moana Beach Park

Just across from the Ala Moana Shopping Center is a beautiful, 76-acre (31-hectare) park with a large, sloping beach offering full facilities and lifeguards. Popular with locals for jogging and family picnics, it's a great alternative to the bustling beaches of Waikiki, and the waters are safe for swimming and boogie-boarding. At the eastern end is the artificial `Aina Moana, or Magic Island, featuring a small, crescent-shaped lagoon at its tip with even calmer waters for smaller children.

Aloha Tower & Marketplace

At 184ft (56m) high, this tower was the tallest building in Hawaii when it was built in 1926 as a harbour control tower for cruise traffic. With four clock faces and a giant 'Aloha' greeting travellers in every direction, it became an instant tourist landmark. The tenth floor has a free Observation Deck offering 360° views of Honolulu (*open: 9am–5pm*). Take a stroll along the shops or watch the ships from the terrace of a waterfront restaurant.
Pier 9, Honolulu Harbor. Tel: (808) 528-5700. www.alohatower.com

Hawaii Maritime Center

Adjacent to the Aloha Tower is this museum examining Hawaii's seafaring history, from the earliest Polynesian settlers and ancient Hawaiian canoes to Pacific whalers and modern surfers, as well as an exhibit on the Hokule`a, a 1976 reconstruction of an open Polynesian canoe which was used to retrace the earliest voyages using traditional methods of stellar navigation. *The Falls of Clyde*, built in 1878 and the world's last surviving full-rigged, four-masted sailing ship, is permanently moored alongside as a museum ship.
Pier 7, Honolulu Harbor. Tel: (808) 536-6373. www.holoholo.org/maritime. Open: 8.30am–5pm. Closed: Christmas. Admission charge. Bus: 19, 20.

Shopping centres

Several large shopping centres range along Ala Moana Boulevard, containing most of Honolulu's shopping and restaurants, outside of Waikiki (*see 'Shopping' p141*).

The *Falls of Clyde* at the Hawaii Maritime Center

Walk: Chinatown

The first Chinese settlers came to Hawaii in 1789 and the bustling streets of Chinatown were home to their descendants for generations. Once notorious as Honolulu's red-light district but undergoing a revitalisation project, it still has a few seedy bars and tattoo parlours mixed in with the trendy art galleries and restaurants.

Approximately 1 mile (1.5km). Allow 2–3 hours minimum.

Begin at the Hawaii Theatre at 1130 Bethel Street, at the corner of Pauahi Street.

1 Hawaii Theatre

This beautiful 1922 Art Deco theatre is listed on the National Historic Register. To see inside, call for weekly tour times (*tel: (808) 528-0506*) or consult the website (*www.hawaiitheatre.com*) or box office for a schedule of performances.

Walk south on Bethel to North Hotel Street and turn right.

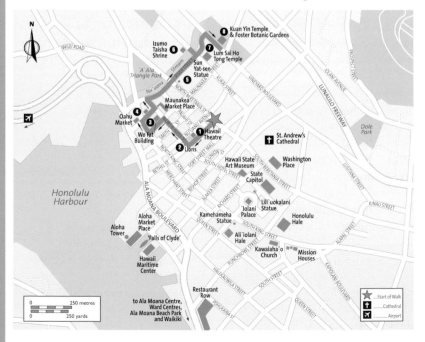

2 Marble lions

Twin marble lions mark Chinatown's official entrance. They were donated by Kaohsiung, Taiwan (Honolulu's sister city), to celebrate the 200th anniversary of Chinese settlement here.

Continue along North Hotel three blocks to Maunakea Street. Turn left on Maunakea, then right on North King Street and walk one block to Kekaulike Street.

3 Food markets

In the mornings, the Oahu Market on the southwest corner of North King and Kekaulike is a frenzy of activity, with fresh fish, meats, fruits and vegetables snapped up by chefs and locals alike. Cross North King and walk up the pedestrian-only section of Kekaulike for more fruit stands, then cross Hotel into Maunakea Marketplace for the best fast-food lunches in Chinatown.

Follow North Hotel for one block to the Nu`uanu Stream, then turn right and head up River Street.

4 Dr Sun Yat-sen Statue

Dr Sun Yat-sen was the first president of the Republic of China. The revolutionary and statesman studied in Hawaii as a teenager and returned many times during his exile from China.

Continue up River Street to Kukui Street. Turn left and cross to the opposite side of the Nu`uanu Stream.

5 Izumo Taisha Shrine

The oldest Japanese Buddhist Shinto shrine in Hawaii was built in 1923 using no nails. It features a large traditional gate and a peace bell presented by the city of Hiroshima.

Return to the east side of the Stream and cross to the north side of Kukui Street.

6 Lum Sai Ho Tong Temple

This small Taoist temple was started in 1899. The present building (1953) features mosaic panels of graceful cranes.

Continue north on River Street to the opposite side of Vineyard Boulevard.

7 Foster Botanical Gardens & Kuan Yin Temple

The gardens on this 14-acre (5.5-hectare) site were first developed in 1853 to preserve native Hawaiian plants. They feature tropical flowers, a 'prehistoric glen' of primitive plants, and a *bo* tree (*Ficus religiosa*) descended from Buddha's Bodhi Tree in India. The serene Buddhist temple (*open: 8.30am–2pm*) located immediately adjacent is the oldest surviving Chinese temple in Hawaii.

50 North Vineyard Blvd. Tel: (808) 522-7066. www.honolulu.gov/parks/hbg. Open: 9am–4pm, tours Mon–Sat 1pm. Closed: New Year, Christmas. Admission charge.

To visit the sights of Downtown Honolulu, walk back down to Beretania Street, turn left and head east for about 5–10 minutes. To return to Waikiki, walk back down to Hotel Street and catch the 2, 13 or B bus.

WAIKIKI

Waikiki was once nothing more than marshy waterfront lands filled with taro fields and fish-ponds. Now it's a huge congregation of high-rise hotels, upscale shops, family restaurants, tourist crowds and one of the world's most famous beaches, all watched over silently by Diamond Head, the ancient volcanic crater to the south.

Most tourists stay at least one night in Waikiki; most of Oahu's accommodation choices are located here, primarily on the streets between **Kalakaua Avenue** at the beachfront and **Kuhio Avenue** one block north (where Waikiki's buses run). It's also where you'll find most of the area's shopping, in storefronts or the crafts-centric **International Marketplace** (which has a large food court for a quick, cheap bite), the upscale **Royal Hawaiian Shopping Center** and the somewhat twee 19th-century-styled **King's Village**.

The centre of Waikiki Beach is unofficially acknowledged as the part beside the **statue of Duke Kahanamoku** (*see text box*), strewn with flower *leis* by day and flanked by flaming torches at night. The gentle, rolling waves here are perfect for beginners' surfing, and in the evenings *hula* dancers and musicians perform. To the west of the statue are two of Hawaii's oldest and finest hotels:

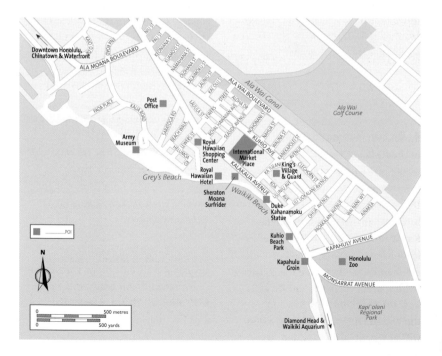

The statue of Duke Kahanamoku welcomes visitors to Waikiki

Just beyond the park is **Diamond Head**, one of Honolulu's best-known landmarks. The tuff cone stands 762ft (232m) high and was created in just days by a volcanic vent blast around 200,000 years ago. Ancient Hawaiians called it *Le`ahi* ('fire headland', after the beacon fires lit to guide canoes), but English sailors in the 19th century mistook worthless calcite crystals for diamonds and the new name stuck. In the 20th century it became a military outpost for harbour defence. A hot and moderately strenuous hike up to the rim (^{2}/₃ mile/1km) offers a splendid panoramic view of Honolulu and Waikiki. Bring sturdy shoes, a hat, water and a torch for the military bunker tunnels you'll need to walk through (*off Diamond Head Road, between Makapu`u and 18th Ave. www.hawaii.gov/dlnr/dsp/oahu.html. Open: 6am–6pm. Admission and parking fees. Bus: 22, 58*).

the classic, white **Sheraton Moana Surfrider** (1901) and 'the pink palace' of the **Royal Hawaiian** (1927). Their lobbies are worth a peek. Walking east from the statue you come to **Kuhio Beach**, where several walls and breakwaters (the largest being the **Kapahulu Groin**) create sheltered lagoons that are safe places for children. Beyond that are the 200 acres (81 hectares) of **Kapi`olani Park**, home to the **Honolulu Zoo** and the **Waikiki Aquarium** (*see p149*) as well as jogging paths and tennis courts.

THE ULTIMATE BEACH BOY

A Waikiki native and one of Hawaii's best-loved sons, Duke Kahanamoku (1890–1968) was a world-champion swimmer and surfer, the first to become inducted into both sports' halls of fame. In 1911, he swam 100m freestyle in Honolulu Harbor in 55.4 seconds, beating the world record by 4.6 seconds, a feat which the Amateur Athletic Union denied as being humanly possible. He won the US five Olympic swimming medals (three gold, two silver) and once surfed a single 35-ft (11-m) wave for a record 1¼ miles (2km).

The USS *Missouri*, site of the Japanese surrender of World War II

PEARL HARBOR

Perhaps the only area of Hawaii more famous than Waikiki is Pearl Harbor, site of the 1941 Japanese attack that drew the US into World War II (*see p44*). Generally considered the finest natural harbour in the Pacific, Kamehameha I appreciated its strategic location and bounteous supply of oysters farmed for their pearls. It later became a supply port for whaling ships and was leased to the US in the 1880s, who first used it as a military outpost for missions to the Philippines during the Spanish-American War. Today it holds Hawaii's largest military base and also serves as a national memorial and historical military park.

USS *Arizona* Memorial

The most popular site at Pearl Harbor is the ivory memorial permanently moored above this sunken battleship. Admission is free, but, with about 4,500 visitors per day, it's important to queue up for tickets as early as possible; they're usually gone by early afternoon. A short film precedes the quick ferry ride to the memorial, where you can gaze down at the ship and view the names of the dead inscribed in marble, most of whom are still entombed below decks just beneath your feet. As a military memorial, respectful dress (no bathing suits or 'profane T-shirts') is required. Note: No bags of any kind are allowed at the memorial; wear or carry your camera and other valuables in your pockets. If you can't carry your valuables, don't leave them in a parked car; pay lockers are available nearby. *6 miles (9.5km) west of Honolulu. Tel: (808) 422-0561. www.nps.gov/usar. Open: 7.30am–5pm, tours 8am–3pm. Closed: New Year, Thanksgiving & Christmas. Free admission. Bus: 20.*

USS *Bowfin* Submarine Museum and Park

Assuming you have a few hours' wait for the USS *Arizona* Memorial – and you don't have a debilitating fear of enclosed spaces – you can check out this former World War II submarine that's berthed just alongside. A self-guided audio tour takes you through the submarine itself, while outside in the park are various World War II-era missiles and torpedoes. You can also purchase a combined admission ticket to the USS *Missouri*. *Tel: (808) 423-1341. www.bowfin.org. Open: 8am–5pm, tickets sold until 2.30pm. Closed: New Year, Thanksgiving & Christmas. Admission charge.*

USS *Missouri*

The last operational battleship in the world, the USS *Missouri* saw action as recently as the first Gulf War, but it's most famous for having been the location of the official Japanese surrender in 1945. Military buffs can explore the decommissioned ship by themselves or pay extra for guided tours. *Tel: (808) 973-2494. www.ussmissouri.org. Open: 9am–5pm, tickets sold until 4pm. Closed: New Year, Thanksgiving, Christmas. Admission charge.*

Names of the dead at the USS *Arizona* Memorial

Honolulu and Oahu

GREATER HONOLULU

The areas to the north and west of downtown hold some of Honolulu's greatest cultural and natural treasures, including top-notch museums, botanical gardens, hiking trails and a resplendent military cemetery located in the crater of an extinct volcano.

Bishop Museum

Housing the finest collection of art and artefacts of Polynesian and Hawaiian history and anthropology, the Bishop Museum began in 1889 with the personal collection of Princess Bernice Pauahi, the last direct descendant of Kamehameha the Great. Hawaii's only planetarium is also located here, with daily shows and combination tickets available.

1525 Bernice St, 2 miles (3km) northwest of downtown. Tel: (808) 847-3511. www.bishopmuseum.org. Open: 9am–5pm. Closed: Christmas. Admission charge. Bus: 2.

The Contemporary Museum

Hawaii's only museum dedicated to contemporary art is housed in a lovely 1925 country estate with beautiful gardens and fantastic views down the hillside to the city below. The on-site café offers excellent lunches.

2411 Makiki Heights Drive. Tel: (808) 526-1322. www.tcmhi.org. Open: Tue–Sat 10am–4pm, Sun noon–4pm. Closed: Mon & most major holidays. Admission charge. Bus: 15.

Hiking trails

Discussed in 'Getting away from it all' (see p120).

Honolulu Academy of Arts and Shangri La

Hawaii's finest museum of arts has 30 galleries featuring an impressive selection of European and American paintings, works from Hawaii and the South Pacific, and a particularly fine collection of East Asian art, including prints and ceramic, bronze and jade craftworks.

Tours leave from here for Shangri La, the exquisite vacation home of American tobacco heiress Doris Duke, which comprises one of the world's largest collections of Islamic art and architecture. Reserve tickets well in advance.

The Bishop Museum has the world's largest collection of Hawaiian artefacts

900 S Beretania St. Tel: (808) 532-8700.
www.honoluluacademy.org,
www.shangrilahawaii.org. Open:
Tue–Sat 10am–4.30pm, Sun 1–5pm.
Closed: New Year, 4 July, Thanksgiving,
Christmas. Admission charge. Bus: 2, 13.

Lyon Arboretum

These lush botanical gardens sit on
more than 190 acres (77 hectares) of
once-deforested land that was
reclaimed by the University of Hawaii.
Shady hiking trails of varying lengths
and difficulty meander through a
tropical rainforest containing more
than 5,000 plant species, including
gorgeous native flowers and several
hundred varieties of palm trees, a
waterfall and at least a dozen types of
local birds. Sturdy shoes with good
traction should be worn; maps can be
downloaded from the website.
3860 Manoa Road. Tel: (808) 988-0464.
www.hawaii.edu/lyonarboretum. Open:
Mon–Fri 9am–4pm. Closed: Sat, Sun &
public holidays. Free admission. Bus: 5.

National Memorial Cemetery of the Pacific

The Punchbowl Crater is an extinct
volcanic caldera that was formed over
75,000 years ago. Once used by the
Hawaiians as a place for human sacrific,
it's grimly apt that today it is a 116-acre
(47-hectare) military cemetery to more
than 25,000 of the nation's soldiers
from various Pacific wars and Vietnam.
The graves of the first Hawaiian
astronaut, Ellison Onizuka (killed in

The American flag flies at half-mast at the
National Memorial Cemetery of the Pacific

the 1986 *Challenger* space shuttle
explosion), and legendary Honolulu
tattoo artist Sailor Jerry are also located
here. It also features amazing views of
Honolulu and Waikiki.
2177 Puowaina Drive. Tel: (808) 532-
3720. Open: 8am–5.30pm Oct–Feb,
8am–6.30pm Mar–Sept. Free admission.
Bus: 15.

The story of Pearl Harbor

In 1941, war raged in Europe and Asia. The Germans occupied much of Europe and were moving into Soviet Russia, while the Japanese cut a swath of destruction across Southeast Asia. American attempts at diplomatic negotiations had failed, and entry into hostilities seemed unavoidable, although Washington wanted Japan to make the first move.

Indeed, for months the Japanese had been preparing for a pre-emptive strike on Pearl Harbor, home of the US Pacific Fleet, with the intent of neutralising US naval power in the Pacific, at least temporarily. Given the inferior strength of their navy, surprise was the most essential part of the plan. Intelligence on the ships, planes and personnel at Pearl Harbor and military airfields around Oahu was undertaken by Japanese spies (some in the Consular Office), and Japanese pilots were trained in an area with similar geography on the island of Kyushu.

On 26 November, a 33-vessel attack fleet, including six aircraft carriers and over 400 planes, sailed from Japan, far from shipping lanes and under strict radio silence. Although US military warnings about possible attacks were sent out, the Philippines or Guam were believed the likely targets, and command in Pearl Harbor earmarked only the southwest for reconnaissance. But by the morning of 7 December, the fleet was in position 230 miles (370km) to the northwest of Oahu.

The first wave of 183 planes reached Pearl Harbor just before 8am, with perfect visibility and seven of the fleet's nine battleships anchored in neat pairs below. The US fleet was utterly unprepared for an attack, with weapons and ammunition secured and no troops on alert. Pearl Harbor and several Navy and Air Force airfields around the island – where the planes had been parked wing-to-wing for storage and were sitting targets – suffered heavy bombing. Many soldiers rallied to defence as best they could, including Doris 'Dorie' Miller, an African-American serving as Mess Attendant on the USS *West Virginia* who dragged his wounded captain to safety and shot down several Japanese planes with an anti-aircraft machine gun despite having no training, acts which later earned him the Navy Cross.

By 10am the attack was over. Eighteen warships (including 8 battleships and 3 destroyers) were sunk, 164 planes destroyed and 128 more damaged, while Japan lost only 29 aircraft and 5 midget submarines. A total of 2,335 military personnel were killed and 1,178 wounded. The battleship USS *Arizona* suffered the heaviest losses; a bomb set off its forward magazine, sinking it in minutes and killing 1,177 servicemen still aboard. Ten hours later, another Japanese fleet attacked an airfield in the Philippines and destroyed numerous parked aircraft. The next day, the US officially entered World War II.

Despite the heavy American losses in the attack, in the long run Japan suffered more – hundreds of thousands dead at Hiroshima and Nagasaki and Japan's utter defeat. Most of the ships damaged or sunk at Pearl Harbor were soon raised, refitted and returned to active service – only the *Arizona* and the *Utah* were lost – while just two of the 33 Japanese ships involved that day survived the war.

The USS *Arizona* Memorial stands above the ship sunk in the Pearl Harbor attack

THE NORTH SHORE

Driving north through the central plains takes you to Oahu's fabled North Shore, home of the picturesque Waimea Valley and some of the greatest surfing in the world. In winter the seas are too dangerous for anyone besides the experts, but in summer the waters are calm enough for swimming and snorkelling. Hale`iwa, the largest town on the North Shore and the centre of Oahu's surfing scene, is good for a meal and a stroll through the shops. Highway 83 continues around through the small beachside towns and valleys of the windward coast, and makes a pleasant return route to Honolulu.

Beaches

The North Shore has some beautiful beaches that are safe for swimming in summer, but from October through April, stick to the shoreline and watch the daredevils catch the waves at famous local breaks like the Banzai Pipeline. **Hale`iwa Beach County Park** is just outside town past the bridge, and further up the road at the base of the valley is **Waimea Bay Beach County Park**, where adventurous types like to jump from the top of a tall rock just off shore. Just after Waimea Bay, the coastline turns into a long string of surfing beaches in quick succession: **Pupukea Beach County Park**, which has fantastic snorkelling and diving around the reefs of submerged lava tubes at **Shark's Cove** (at its eastern end), **`Ehukai Beach County Park** and the postcard-pretty **Sunset Beach**.

Hale`iwa

This former plantation town is now a surfing mecca and hippie hub with a small-town charm. The main road is dotted with cafés and restaurants, an

Surfboards for sale in Hale`iwa

Waimea Bay Beach Country Park

organic food store, gift shops, art galleries and surf shops, and though it caters more for locals, there's enough to enjoy for those just passing through. Be sure to stop by Matsumoto's, a Japanese grocery store renowned for its shave ices.

Pu`u O Mahuka Heiau State Monument

Set at the top of the ridge overlooking Waimea Valley are the ruins of what was once the island's largest *heiau luakini* (temple of human sacrifice). While impressive for their size, even more interesting than the ruins are the views of Waimea Valley and its beach below, and the North Shore coast in the distance – just walk around the *heiau* and follow the red-dirt trails through the tall grass to the edge of the bluff. To get to the monument, turn inland from Highway 83 onto Pupukea Road (at the Foodland supermarket) and follow signs up the hill and over the dirt road to the car park.

Waimea Valley Audubon Center

The Waimea Valley was once home to a thriving Hawaiian settlement. Today it's been preserved as a large, lush botanical centre, with trails meandering through dozens of different gardens of tropical plants where native and introduced birds like *nene* geese and peacocks wander freely. There are also a number of archaeological sites and ancient ruins of *heiaus*, and at the far end of the valley is Waimea Falls, a 60-ft (18-m) double waterfall.

59–864 Kamehameha Highway (Hwy 83), 5 miles (8km) east of Hale`iwa. Tel: (808) 638-9199. waimea.audubon.org. Open: 9.30am–5.30pm. Closed: New Year, Christmas. Admission charge.

SOUTHEAST AND WINDWARD OAHU
Beaches

Many beaches here are generally safe for swimming, but always heed signs and lifeguard warnings. Four miles (6.5km) past Makapu`u Point on Highway 72 is **Waimanalo Beach County Park**, at 3 miles (5km) the longest beach on Oahu, with a beautiful setting and safe swimming and boogie-boarding. About 6½ miles (10.5km) further north, turn right onto Kailua Road to get to Kailua Beach Park, another large and particularly beautiful beach, popular with families, windsurfers and kayakers, with full facilities and equipment hire. For fewer crowds, south along the coast from Kailua Beach is Lanikai Beach, a picturesque white-sand beach stretching 1 mile (1.5km) alongside seaside mansions.

The long and beautiful Waimanalo Beach

Byodo-In temple

A faithful replica of a 900-year-old Japanese temple, built to commemorate the migration of Japanese to Hawaii, this large, red, double-winged structure features a 9-ft (3-m) tall gold Buddha, large koi ponds and a 3-ton bronze 'peace bell'.

Valley of the Temples Memorial Park, 47–200 Kahekili Highway (Hwy 83), Kane`ohe. Tel: (808) 239-8811. Open: 8.30am–4.30pm. Closed: Christmas. Admission charge.

Hanauma Bay Nature Preserve

The large coral reefs just offshore offer the best snorkelling on Oahu and feature tropical fish and sea turtles. The locale's popularity is also its biggest threat – all first-time visitors are required to watch a short film on reef preservation. Snorkelling equipment can be hired, and there are lockers, showers and changing rooms. It's also a pleasant (if slightly crowded) beach for a family picnic; the café is a bit pricey, so it's best to bring your own food.

10 miles (16km) east of Waikiki on Kalaniana`ole Highway (Hwy 72). Tel: (808) 396-4229. www. honolulu.gov/parks/facility/hanaumabay. Open: Mon & Wed–Sun 6am–6pm winter, 6am–7pm summer. Closed: Tue. Admission charge, parking fee, equipment hire. Bus: 22.

Kane`ohe Bay

Lovely Kane`ohe Bay is the largest in Hawaii. Although it has no suitable swimming beaches, you can get a closer (and drier) look at the marine life of its barrier reef by taking a one-hour cruise on the glass-bottom boat *Coral Queen (tel: (808) 235-2888; open: Mon–Sat 10am–1.30pm).*

Makapu`u Point

As the highway rounds Oahu's southeastern tip, look for Makapu`u State Wayside, where a hiking trail (1hr return) winds down to a platform offering scenic views of the lighthouse below, the coastline, and the island of Molokai in the distance. Non-hikers can keep driving to the Makapu`u lookout, where from just off the car park you can see the coastal cliffs to the northwest, some small, uninhabited islands populated by wild rabbits and seabirds, and Makapu`u Beach (unsafe for swimming).

14 miles (22.5km) east of Waikiki on Kalaniana`ole Highway (Hwy 72).

Nu`uanu Pali State Park

The best view of southeastern Oahu can be found here, high up on the inland Pali Highway. It was over these pali (cliffs) that Kamehameha the Great drove his rival's army at the Battle of Nu`uanu Valley in 1795, gaining him control of Oahu. Several hundred skulls were found when the highway was built in the late 19th century. Don't leave valuables in your car here.

Pali Highway (Hwy 61).
Open: 4am–8pm.

Southeastern Oahu from Nu`uanu Pali State Park

Hawai`i, the Big Island

The youngest of the islands is Hawai`i, called 'the Big Island' to avoid confusion with the state as a whole. Not only is it big – bigger than all of the other islands combined – but it's still growing, thanks to an active volcano that continues to reshape the coastline with fresh flows of lava. A truly original destination, its size and amazing climatic diversity means it's got something for everyone, from sun-drenched beaches and hillside cattle pastures to steaming volcanic vents and significant historical sites.

Although it's possible to drive the complete circle of the Hawaii Belt Road (Highway 11) in a day, Hawai`i is really too big to be explored from just one base. It's best to figure out what you'd like to see and base yourself nearby for that portion of your trip. Kailua has the largest choice of accommodations and is closest to the coffee towns of Kona and the southern beaches and central ranchlands of Kohala, while Hilo will let you explore the Hamakua Coast, Volcanoes National Park and the Puna district.

Orientation

Several volcanoes form the bulk of the Big Island: the two biggest are the dormant Mauna Kea (13,796ft/4,205m) in the northeast and the still-active Mauna Loa (13,677ft/4,169m) in the southwest; Kilauea ('much spewing'), traditional home of the volcano goddess Pele, started erupting in 1983 and hasn't yet stopped. The island's

most visited area, the Kona Coast, takes up most of the dry, leeward (western) side of the island, with its prime coffee-growing regions located on the western slopes of Mauna Kea. The rainier, windward (eastern) coast has Hilo, the second-largest town in the state; to its north is the Hamakua Coast, while the small district of Puna juts out to the southeast. The Kohala district is a large, mountainous peninsula located to the north halfway between the leeward and windward coasts.

Much of the sparsely settled southern district of Ka`u is taken up by Mauna Loa and Hawai`i Volcanoes National Park, but trivia lovers everywhere know it as the location of Ka Lae, the southernmost point of land in the United States.

History

Hawai`i was the earliest island to see Polynesian settlement. It was from the northern Kohala district that native son

Kamehameha the Great launched his quest to conquer and unite all of the islands in the chain – his victory assured that the name of 'Hawai`i' would live on as that of the entire kingdom. Other notable events here include the death of Captain Cook in 1779; the death of Kamehameha the Great in 1819 and the abolishment of the ancient *kapu* system by his son Liholiho (King Kamehameha II) later that year; and the arrival of Hawaii's first Christian missionaries in 1820. The first Hawaiian cattle ranch was founded here at Waimea, and although for most of the last two centuries the sugar plantations of Hamakua drove the island's economic engine, today it relies primarily on tourism and specialised crops; the island is the largest American producer of both ginger and premium coffee beans.

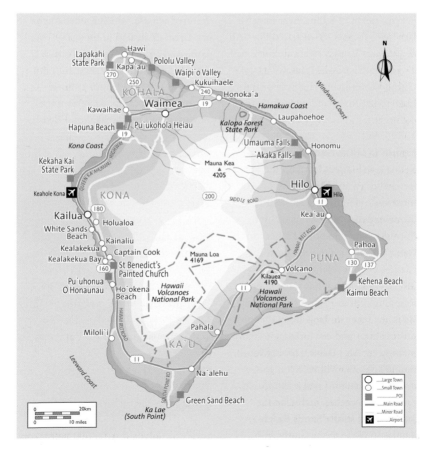

THE KONA COAST

The lengthy leeward coast of the Big Island has long been a site of historical importance; its main town Kailua was both the site of King Kamehameha the Great's court and the home of the first Christian missionaries in the islands. Today it's best known as a favourite haunt of sun-seeking tourists and dedicated coffee lovers making a pilgrimage to the home of Kona coffee, one of the world's finest.

Kona's airport is located 7 miles (11km) north of Kailua, near massive lava fields from a 200-year-old flow. All of the Kona Coast's sights are lined up and down Highway 11, known as Queen Ka`ahumanu Highway or the Hawaii Belt Road, and make for easy day trips.

Kailua (Kailua-Kona)

Kailua is the largest town on the leeward coast and the first stop for most visitors to the Big Island. (The 'Kona' appellation was tagged on to distinguish it from other Kailuas on Oahu and Maui, although most Big Island folk now refer to it simply as 'Kona'.) Although it has some large shopping centres just off the highway, it's much nicer to stroll along the long row of shops and restaurants on its main street **Ali`i Drive**. Driving south on it from town will take you past ocean-front condos and a handful of pretty little beaches, including the pocket-sized **White Sands Beach** 4 miles (6.5km) to the south. Also known as 'Magic Sands' for its propensity to get swept away by winter storms, this beach is popular with families and has the only known *heiau* (temple) dedicated to the ancient sport of surfing.

At the northern end of town you'll find three historical sights symbolising some of the most significant eras of Hawaiian history.

Ahu`ena Heiau

Located at the mouth of the bay is this restored temple, which Kamehameha the Great dedicated to the harvest-god Lono and made his capital from 1812 until his death in 1819. Access to the platform is forbidden for cultural reasons, but it can be seen from the northern end of Kamakahonu Beach.

Kailua Bay from Ali`i Drive

Hawaiian royalty used Hulihe`e Palace as a vacation home

Hulihe`e Palace

This home was built in 1838 for Governor John Adams Kuakini, King Kamehameha's cousin. When he died it became a vacation home for Hawaiian monarchs. The interior, with its preserved 19th-century *koa*-wood furnishings, offers an inside look at the life of Victorian-era Hawaiian royalty. *75-5718 Ali`i Drive. Tel: (808) 329-1877. www.daughtersofhawaii.com. Open: Mon–Sat 9am–4pm, Sun 10am–4pm. Admission charge.*

Moku`aikaua church

Directly across the road from Hulihe`e Palace stands this large, lava-rock church, built in 1837 to replace the first Christian church ever built in the Hawaiian islands, a thatched hut erected in 1820 with the arrival of the first missionaries. A small museum exhibit at one end is devoted to the early history of Christianity in Hawaii, with a model of the missionaries' first ship and reproductions of their personal letters and journals. *Open: daylight hours. Free admission.*

Ho`okena Beach

Around 19 miles (31km) south of Kailua-Kona, a *makai* turn-off leads a few miles down to Kauhauko Bay and Ho`okena Beach Park, a nice-sized

KONA COFFEE

Hawaiian coffee – the only kind grown in the US – is well known as a gourmet brew with a rich, dark flavour, but only beans grown on the leeward slopes of Mauna Loa can be called 'Kona'. As early cultivators discovered, the mountain offers perfect growing conditions for *Coffea arabica*, with morning sunshine, afternoon rains and nutrient-rich volcanic soil. Over 650 independent coffee farms here harvest more than 3.5 million pounds (1,587,600kg) annually – a tiny percentage of the world crop but a large part of the premium market. Coffee lovers can visit in November for the Kona Coffee Cultural Festival, featuring a full schedule of tastings and farm tours.

grey-sand beach backed by seacliffs and shady trees. The diving and snorkelling here are excellent, although footwear is recommended because of the sharp lava rocks. It has toilet facilities and picnic tables, and camping is allowed with a permit from the county parks department.

Kona Coast coffee towns

A drive down Highway 11 from Kailua will take you through small towns where coffee is king and the road is dotted with shops, galleries, restaurants and, naturally, coffee shops. You'll see

The interior of St Benedict's Painted Church

more than a few winsome period buildings, such as the 1930s Aloha Theatre in **Kainaliu** or the 1917 Manago Hotel in **Captain Cook**. The explorer met his end at nearby Kealakekua Bay, although the town of **Kealakekua** (of 'Little Grass Shack' song fame) is actually a bit further north. The **Kona Historical Society** (*www.konahistorical.org*) has a small museum located here in an 1875 general store; they also offer guided walking tours of Kailua and a nearby working coffee farm. On your way back, head inland at the junction of Highway 180 to visit the art galleries of **Holualoa**, located up the mountain's slopes just a few miles south of Kailua.

The royal compound at Pu'uhonua O Honaunau

Pu'uhonua O Honaunau National Historical Park

According to the ancient Hawaiian custom of *kapu* (taboo), the penalty for breaking a law was death. The only chance *kapu*-breakers had for survival was to evade their pursuers and reach the nearest *pu'uhonua* ('place of refuge'), typically located on a rocky coastline or other hard-to-reach place.

The largest *pu'uhonua* on the Big Island was at Honaunau Bay, situated at a royal compound, the remains of which have been restored and preserved as a national park. A self-guided tour map takes you through the thatched huts, outrigger canoes, *heiaus* and carved wooden statues of fierce-looking Hawaiian gods. A large cultural

festival is held here on the last weekend in June.

Highway 160, off Highway 11. Tel: (808) 328-2326. www.nps.gov/puho. Open: 7am–5pm. Visitor Center 8am–5pm. Admission charge.

St Benedict's Painted Church

The entire exterior of this small Catholic church was brightly decorated by a Belgian priest over a century ago. The walls are festooned with biblical scenes, *trompe l'oeil* is used to make the apse look like a European Gothic cathedral, and the pillar tops are turned into palm trees spreading their fronds out against a starry night sky.

Off Highway 160, near Pu'uhonua O Honaunau National Park. Open: daylight hours.

HAWAI`I VOLCANOES NATIONAL PARK

This national park is one of the most singular and popular destinations in all of Hawaii, thanks mostly to the Pu`u `O`o crater, a cinder cone of the active Kilauea Volcano which has been erupting more or less continuously since 1983.

The park covers an area of about 250,000 acres (101,170 hectares) and includes the summit of Mauna Loa and and more than 150 miles (241km) of hiking trails of varying lengths and levels (*see p121*). It's located 100 miles (160km) southeast of Kailua-Kona and 30 miles (48km) southwest of Hilo. A mile or so east of the park entrance is tiny Volcano Village, which has a few restaurants and cafés, gift shops and a service station.

Tel: (808) 985-6000. www.nps.gov/havo. Open: 24 hours a day. Admission charge.

Crater Rim Drive

This road circles 11 miles (18km) around the top of the Kilauea Caldera and has many of the park's sights ranged around it. It's an easy way to see much of the park's attractions if you have a limited amount of time.

The following are listed in the order in which you come to them when driving the loop road.

Kilauea Visitor Center

Typically the first stop for visitors, here you can get a detailed map of the park and find out if any areas are closed due

Volcanic fumes seep up along Crater Rim Drive

to volcanic activity. Also featured are numerous exhibits about the park's preservation efforts, and the ecosystems, geology and fauna of the Big Island. Rangers give educational talks on the half-hour.

Open: 7.45am–5pm.

Jaggar Museum

This museum of volcanology is named for Thomas Jaggar, a professor of geology, widely considered a pioneer of this relatively young science. It was he who founded the Hawaiian Volcano Observatory (*hvo.wr.usgs.gov*) at Kilauea, and in 1916 he helped convince the US government to create the national park. Exhibits explain many of the techniques scientists use to measure things like seismic activity, lava temperature and volcanic gases, and also tell traditional stories of Pele, the fierce goddess of Hawaii's volcanoes. An outdoor overlook offers views over the caldera itself.

Open: 8.30am–5pm.

Halema`uma`u Crater

A short walk from a car park takes you to the lookout point for this crater-within-a-crater, which was created inside the caldera by a fresh eruption in the 19th century (described by Mark Twain as a 'heaving sea of molten fire' during his 1866 visit). Although the crater is now just a dry hole, it still emits sulphuric volcanic fumes, so

it's recommended that those with heart or respiratory problems, pregnant women, infants and small children avoid this area.

Thurston Lava Tube

This giant, underground, smooth-walled tube, located in a forested area of giant ferns and `ohia trees, was once a pipeline for molten lava rushing down to the sea. An easy, 10-minute trail leads to and through the tube.

Chain of Craters Road

This route, which intersects with Crater Rim Drive on the far side of the caldera, offers a 36-mile (58km) round

The gigantic Kilauea Caldera at Hawai`i Volcanoes National Park

trip descending 3,700ft (1,128m) to the coast, where a flow of hardened lava across the road marks its end – it once ran all along the coast to Puna and may be shorter still by the time you get there. But here's where you have the best chance of seeing the white steam plumes and perhaps even fresh-flowing lava from the current eruption, which is even more striking in the afternoon or night when it glows red against the dark. Of course, Kilauea doesn't perform on command, so you'll need to check its current activity on the park website or at the Visitor Center.

Along the road are several craters, hike trailheads and a boardwalk trail to the **Pu`u Loa petroglyphs**, containing ancient Hawaiian rock carvings and holes into which the umbilical cords of newborn infants were slipped for luck and long life. At the end of the road is the **Holei Sea Arch**, a 90-ft-tall (28-m) lava arch formed by ocean erosion. The small ranger station in the car park has information about current lava viewing locations and air quality, and offers (usually hot and humid) guided hikes across the fields, subject to conditions. Enquire at the Visitor Center for the daily schedule. (If you plan to hike, be sure to read the requirements and safety precautions on the website beforehand. Visitors have died here in the past.)

Make sure your car has enough petrol before taking this road, as there are no facilities of any kind along the way, and even the service stations in Volcano Village close by nightfall.

Mauna Loa as seen from the Southwest Rift

HILO AND AROUND

Hilo is the state's 'second city', home to over 40,000 residents and its own University of Hawaii campus, although with its often overcast and drizzly windward-coast weather, it's a far cry from the postcard-perfect skies of Honolulu.

But Hilo has plenty of distinctive charm to recommend it for a visit – a pleasantly vintage downtown, filled with historic buildings, some beautiful parks, a number of fine museums, and the close proximity of the beautiful Hamakua Coast and Hawaii Volcanoes National Park.

Lyman Mission House

Farmers' Market

Every Wednesday and Saturday, a farmers' market and crafts fair is held in downtown Hilo, at the corner of Kamehameha Avenue and Mamo Street. The stalls feature a good selection of clothing, jewellery, handicrafts, tropical fruits and flowers, coffee beans and other Hawaiiana.

'Imiloa Astronomy Center

Hilo's newest attraction is this strikingly designed, multi-million-dollar astronomy museum and planetarium, with three giant cone-shaped roofs in honour of the three largest mountains on the island. The display and multimedia exhibits inside interpret the natural history of Maunakea through both scientific enquiry and the traditional Hawaiian creation chants, as well as exploring the place of astronomy in the lives of the Hawaiians and their seafaring Polynesian ancestors. A planetarium features state-of-the-art A/V presentations and an upscale café offers clear views down to Hilo's bay.

600 'Imiloa Place (off Komohana and Nowelo Sts). Tel: (808) 969-9700. www.imiloahawaii.org. Open: Tue–Sun 9am–4pm. Closed: Mon, New Year, Thanksgiving, Christmas. Admission charge.

Lyman Museum and Mission House

The Lyman is a multi-gallery museum featuring exhibits on the natural history, ecosystems and geology of the Big Island; the cultural heritage of the people of Hawaii; 19th- and 20th-century works of art by Hawaiian

Pacific Tsunami Museum

Sarah Lyman. Viewable by guided tour, it contains much of its original furniture and housewares.

276 Haili St, Kapi`olani. Tel: (808) 935-5021. www.lymanmuseum.org. Open: Mon–Sat 9.30am–4.30pm; Mission House tours: 11am, 1pm, 3pm. Closed: Sun, public holidays. Admission charge.

Mokupapapa Discovery Center

This large storefront museum, located in the historic S Hate Building (*see p63*), contains traditional and multimedia displays all about the Papahanaumokuakea Marine National Monument, a federally protected swath of ocean covering about 138,000sq miles (357,500sq km). The largest marine conservation area in the world, it contains the multitudes of uninhabited islands, atolls, shoals and coral reefs that make up the

artists; and a large collection of Chinese art and artefacts. Immediately adjacent is the Mission House, built in 1839 for New England missionaries (and museum founder forebears) David and

---

TSUNAMI TOWN

Tsunami is Japanese for 'harbour wave', and Hilo, the 'tsunami capital', has suffered more from these destructive ocean events than anywhere else in Hawaii. Several causes contribute: the bay faces north, towards the extremely earthquake-prone Aleutian Islands; the bay's funnel shape directs incoming waves right towards town; and the 'seiche' effect of water moving naturally back and forth in the bay can amplify the tsunami waves. The catastrophic tsunamis of 1946 and 1960 together killed almost 200 people around Hilo and resulted in millions of dollars of destruction. After the bayfront Japanese neighbourhood Shinmachi was thus destroyed twice in 15 years, the area was transformed into Wailoa River State Park.

Northwestern Hawaiian Islands, home to more than 7,000 marine species including endangered green sea turtles and monk seals, seabirds and tropical fish, some of which can be seen in the museum's gigantic aquarium.

308 Kamehameha Ave. Tel: (808) 933-8184. www.hawaiireef.noaa.gov. Open: Tue–Sat 9am–4pm. Closed: Sun, Mon, federal holidays. Free admission.

Pacific Tsunami Museum

This small but comprehensive museum explains the history and scientific phenomenon of tsunamis worldwide, around Hawaii, and in Hilo in particular. Archival photographs and videotaped survivor interviews make for compelling and poignant tales, such as the young teacher who survived eight hours floating on debris after being washed away from nearby Laupahoehoe Point.

130 Kamehameha Ave (at Kalakaua St). Tel: (808) 935-0926. www.tsunami.org. Open: Mon–Sat 9am–4pm. Closed: Sun, New Year, Thanksgiving, Christmas Eve, Christmas Day. Admission charge.

Rainbow Falls and Boiling Pots

Aptly named, these 80-ft (24-m) waterfalls on the Wailuku River, just a short drive from downtown Hilo, often create beautiful rainbows when the sun hits the spray. Behind the falls is a large cave that legend says was the home of Hina, mother of the Hawaiian god Maui, who pulled all the islands out of the ocean with his fishing hook. About 1½ miles (2.5km) further along the road are the Boiling Pots, a series of roiling pools of water created by the river's descent towards the ocean.

Off Waianuenue Ave, 2 miles (3km) west of downtown.

Rainbow Falls

Walk: Bayside Hilo

This walk takes you past some of Hilo's classic downtown buildings and ends with a walk along the bay to beautiful Japanese gardens.

4 miles (6.5km). Allow 2 hours.

Start on the left side of Kalakaua Ave just north of Keawe St.

1 Hawaiian Telephone Building
Possibly the prettiest public-utility building anywhere, this 1920s gem was designed by famed architect C W Dickey, and combines influences from Spanish, Italian, Californian and traditional Hawaiian designs.
Cross the street into the park.

2 Kalakaua Park
This grassy plaza features a lily pool and a gigantic banyan tree standing over a bronze statue of King David Kalakaua holding taro leaves and an *ipu* (gourd percussion instrument) to symbolise, respectively, his connection to the land and to the cultural arts he helped revive. Across the park is the grand 1919 Federal Building.
Turn right onto Waianuenue Ave and walk to the corner.

3 Burns Hotel and Toyama Building
The 1911 Burns Hotel on the corner is now the Hilo Bay Hostel. Across the

street is the 1908 Toyama Building, a former Masonic Hall which has been restored and now contains one of Hilo's best restaurants.
Walk one block down Waianuenue to Kamehameha Ave.

4 F W Koehnen Building
Stretching to the southeast, Kamehameha Avenue is lined with some of Hilo's oldest storefronts. The large building on the western corner was built in 1910 as a saddle store, but has housed Koehnen's home furnishings since 1957. Step inside to see vintage photographs and beautiful `ohia floors and *koa* cabinets. Upstairs has fantastic views of the bay.
Walk southeast along Kamehameha Ave.

5 Kress Building and Palace Theater
You'll pass the Pacific Tsunami Museum (*see p61*), housed in a C W Dickey-designed bank from 1930. On the next block is the Art Deco Kress Building

(1932), once a department store and now a cinema complex. Detour briefly up Haili Street to see the Palace Theater (1925), the Big Island's first deluxe playhouse, which today shows movies and live performances.
Continue walking along Kamehameha Ave.

6 S Hate Building

This large 1912 building was erected by Sadanosuke Hate, a Japanese dry-goods merchant. During World War II, the family was sent to an internment camp and the building confiscated by the US government. Hate's daughter had to buy it back after the war for $100,000.
Cross Kamehemeha Ave at the bus station and turn right to continue on through the park.

7 Bayfront Beach Park and Wailoa River State Park

This long park follows the curve of the bayside breakwater built in the early 20th century to provide Hilo with a safe port. Wailoa River State Park (*see box p60*) is to the south.
Continue walking along the bay to Manono St. and turn left.

8 Lili`uokalani Gardens and Banyan Drive

Designed in the Japanese style, the gardens feature stone bridges, graceful trees and rock-lined ponds. Stretching away to the east is Banyan Drive, lined with old hotels and majestic banyans planted less than 100 years ago by notable historic figures.

Walk: Bayside Hilo

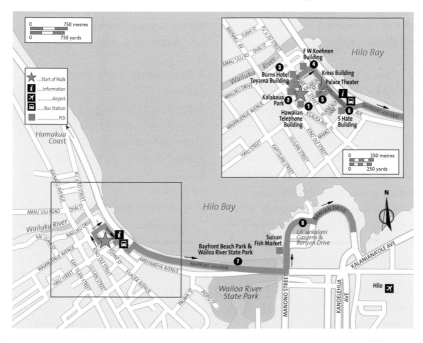

Drive: The 'Red Road' of Puna

This drive follows the spectacular coastline along Puna's Highway 137, which was once paved with crushed red lava rocks.

Around 33 miles (53km). Allow at least half a day.

Start at Pahoa on Highway 130 and continue south for about 8 miles (13km).

1 'Star of the Sea' Painted Church

This tiny 1930s church stands on the site of the first Hawaiian mission of Father Damien of Molokai (*see p118*). The interior is colourfully painted with *trompe l'oeil* and biblical allegories and features stained-glass windows of Father Damien and Mother Marianne Cope.
Open: 9am–4pm.

2 Kaimu Beach

Just down the road is all that's left of the towns of Kalapana and Kaimu, which where swallowed by massive lava flows in the early 1990s; only Verna's Café (*open: 10am–5pm*) survived. An easy, unshaded 5-minute walk across the lava brings you to what's left of Kaimu Beach, where the jet-black sands are a stunning contrast to the thrashing surf.
From Kaimu, head east (straight ahead) on Highway 137 for 3½ miles (5.5km).

3 Kehena Beach

This stunning little black-sand beach – at the bottom of a rocky hillside path –

is popular with locals, who often go nude. Dolphins sometimes swim by in the mornings. If the water is calm, it's generally safe to take a dip, but stay close to shore and mind the currents. Further down the road is the Kalani Oceanside Retreat (*see pp164–5*), which offers a vegetarian-friendly, organic-food buffet lunch from noon to 1pm.

4 MacKenzie State Recreational Area

Pass through the village of Opihikao and you'll come to this clifftop park.
Continue for 2 miles (3km).
At the T-junction, turn right (towards Kapoho).

5 Isaac Hale Beach Park

This popular local family beach features strong waves; it's safer if you stay close to the protected boat ramp.

6 Ahalanui Beach Park

A little further along is a large lagoon pool, fed by naturally heated spring water and separated from the ocean by a low rock wall. It's popular with families and has lifeguards and showers. *Continue along Highway 137. Take the first right turn onto Kapoho Kai Drive, follow it to the end and turn left on Waiopae Street.*

7 Wai`opae Tide Pools

Located just off a small suburb of vacation homes at Kapoho Point, these shallow lava-rock pools offer great snorkelling and safe swimming. Wear reef shoes to protect your feet.

Return to Highway 137 and turn right. At the four-way intersection, turn left and head west on Highway 132.

8 Lava Tree State Monument

An easy trail loops through this forest filled with strangely shaped lava columns. *Continue along Highway 132 to the main street of Pahoa.*

9 Pahoa

Pahoa has a small main street with a few false-front cafés.

Drive: The 'Red Road' of Puna

KOHALA AND THE NORTH

Large parts of the Kohala area were once entirely inaccessible due to lava flows, but the sunny leeward beaches were too beautiful for developers to resist, and it now hosts a string of resort hotels. Kamehameha the Great was born in Kohala, and his legacy is everywhere, most significantly at the giant *heiau* he built here. *Mauka* are the cool, green uplands of the Kohala Mountains, where Hawaii's oldest cattle ranch still operates around the central town of Waimea.

Highway 19 takes you past the beaches and straight on to Waimea, while highways 270 (along the coast) and 250 (across the mountain ridge) make an easy loop around the peninsula – a very pleasant day trip, especially if you stop in the small towns of Hawi and Kapa̖'au.

The main street of Kapa̖'au is filled with quaint old stores

Hapuna Beach

A broad expanse of white sand and safe waters makes this one of the island's most popular beaches, with good swimming, snorkelling and boogie-boarding. Although a large hotel dominates the northern end, there's plenty of room for everyone. A state park, it has full facilities including lifeguards and washrooms, and the snack bar hires out beach equipment. *Off Highway 19, 4 miles (6.5km) south of Kawaihae. Open: 7am–8pm.*

Hawi and Kapa̖'au

Like so many other former plantation towns in the islands, Hawi and Kapa̖'au had to reinvent themselves when the sugar mills closed. Today they boast charming main streets lined with brightly painted wooden storefronts containing all manner of shops and cafés. Hawi, at the junction of highways 250 and 270, has some nice places to eat, including a delicious bakery. Two miles (3km) further on, Kapa̖'au has several art galleries and an excellent bookshop, as well as the original statue of Kamehameha the Great that was temporarily lost at sea and later found (the one in Honolulu was a replica commissioned with the insurance money).

Lapakahi State Historical Park

A large Hawaiian settlement thrived along sheltered Koai̖'e Cove for 500 years before being abandoned in the 19th century. A self-guided (and

Pu`ukohola Heiau, where Kamehameha the Great sacrificed his enemies

unshaded) 1-mile (1.5-km) loop trail leads through the ruins; a brochure describes village life and explains the functions of various houses, temples, canoe enclosures and even artefacts like a stone board for playing *konane* (draughts).

Highway 270, 12 miles (19km) north of Kawaihae. Open: 8am–4pm. Closed: state holidays. Free admission.

Pololu Valley

Highway 270 ends at the island's northern tip with a striking viewpoint of the valley. A moderately difficult trek down a rocky, 1-mile (1.5-km) trail leading to an ironwood grove and a black-sand beach offers stunning views down the coast.

Pu`ukohola Heiau National Historic Site and Spencer Beach

This giant temple was built to honour the personal war god of Kamehameha the Great during his quest to conquer the Hawaiian islands. Its inaugural human sacrifice was Keoua, a rival chief from the south, who was invited to the opening ceremonies and killed as he stepped ashore.

Pu`ukohola is one of the largest *heiau* in the islands, and the last one ever to be built, since the Hawaiian religion was dismantled just three decades later. The massive structure, made with black lava rocks, stands on the crest of a hill overlooking the sea. Nearby are smaller *heiaus*, including one submerged in the bay and dedicated to shark gods (sacrifices were graciously accepted by their earthly counterparts). A quick drive up the highway takes you to the homestead of John Young, a stranded British sailor who became a close personal advisor to Kamehameha and later the governor of the Big Island. Immediately to the south is **Spencer Beach County Park**, ringed by knotty old trees and sheltered by a long reef offshore. The swimming is very safe, and it's popular with families and campers.

Pu`ukohola. Highway 270, ¼ mile (0.4km) north of Highway 19 intersection. Tel: (808) 882-7218. www.nps.gov/puhe. Open: 7.30am–4pm. Free admission.

Waimea and Parker Ranch

This large ranch town (also known as Kamuela), sits on rolling pasture land 2,700ft (820m) above sea level, giving it some of the coolest temperatures on the Big Island. It has several shopping centres.

The town's backbone is **Parker Ranch**, built by an English sailor under charter from Kamehameha himself. It still maintains around 60,000 head of cattle on 150,000 acres (60,000 hectares). The Visitor Center, located at the Parker Ranch Shopping Center, has archival footage and artefacts from 19th-century *paniolo* life, and a shop with all manner of cowboy-themed items. The ranch also offers tours of two historic homes, ATV (all-terrain vehicle) and horseback rides.

Parker Ranch Shopping Center. Highway 19. Tel: (808) 885-7655. www.parkerranch.com. Open: Mon–Sat 9am–4.45pm. Closed: Sun, public holidays. Admission charge.

A statue in Waimea celebrates Hawaii's cowboy culture

THE HAMAKUA COAST

The 50 miles (80km) of coast north of Hilo, sloping down from the mighty summit of Mauna Kea, feature some of the Big Island's prettiest windward scenery, with deep, verdant valleys, imposing waterfalls and rocky shorelines. Everything is easily accessible and well signed from Highway 19, which runs past former sugar-mill towns and across old railroad bridges ranging over narrow ravines cut by mountain streams rushing down to the sea.

The majestic `Akaka Falls

`Akaka Falls

One of the Big Island's most photographed sites is this majestic waterfall located about 3½ miles (5.5km) west of the little town of **Honomu**, off Highway 19. Plummeting 420ft (130m) down from a moss-lined cliff in a wide chasm, its lookout is always full of tourists but makes for a worthwhile photo opportunity regardless. A short path from the car park takes you directly to `Akaka, or you can extend your walk to include the half-hour loop trail that will take in the nearby **Kahuna Falls** (400ft/120m) as well. Honomu, a former sugar town, is now a rest stop for visitors, with several cafés and gift shops, including the Ishigo General Store, built in 1910 and still run by the same family.

Honoka`a

If you plan to visit Waipi`o Valley, you'll pass through Honoka`a, the largest of

the Hamakua Coast sugar towns. Its main street has some appealing classic storefronts, many of them wooden falsefronts, including the 1930 Honoka`a People's Theater and the 1927 Hamakau branch of the Bank of Hawaii, as well as some antique and junk shops to browse through.

Kalopa Native Forest State Park

Five miles (8km) south of Honoka`a, an inland turn takes you 2,000ft (610m) up the slopes of Mauna Kea to this rich and cool-climate forest reserve, a favourite camping site for locals that's all too often ignored by tourists. An easy ¾-mile (1.25-km) loop trail winds through a forest of native flora such as *koa*, *ohi`a* and *kopiko* trees; you may even see the `*io* (Hawaiian hawk) or the tiny `*elepaio*, a bird closely watched by

View from the Pepe'ekeo Scenic Drive

ancient *kahunas* (priests) selecting koa trees for canoes – if any were seen pecking at the bark, it meant the tree was full of insects and the wood would therefore be unusable.

Laupahoehoe

Laupahoehoe ('leaf of lava', pronounced *LAW-pa-hoy-hoy*) is a coastal village ranged along a rocky outcrop. Its picturesque location proved tragic in 1946, when a great tsunami swept over the school at the headland's tip, killing 24 students and teachers. A video interview with the lone surviving teacher can be seen at Hilo's Pacific Tsunami Museum (*see p61*).
The tsunami also wiped out the nearby sugar mills' rail line, which ran through the town.

Laupahoehoe Point Road, a *makai* (oceanward) turn off Highway 19 to the north of the promontory, winds tightly down to the headland's park, which offers memorable views of seacliffs and pounding surf.

Pepe'ekeo Scenic Drive

Several miles north of Hilo, a 'scenic drive' (as it is signposted) turn-off from Highway 19 leads you down this lovely, 4-mile (6.5-km) road that was once the original Mamalahoa Highway. It leads through lush, overhanging trees, past tiny scalloped bays (a roadside trail offers shoreline access), and is absolutely worth a detour. Halfway along the road is the **Hawaii Tropical Botanical Garden**, a nature preserve offering a self-guided tour through the tropical rainforest and down to lovely Onomea Bay.

Hawaii Tropical Botanical Garden. Tel: (808) 964-5233. www.htbg.com. Open: 9am–4pm. Admission charge.

Waipi`o Valley

At the end of Highway 240, which spurs off north from Highway 19 as it rounds to the coast, you'll find the stunning and culturally significant Waipi`o Valley, the largest in the chain of seven amphitheatre valleys that march across the island's northern coast. It's a full mile (1.5km) wide at its mouth and stretches back 6 miles (10km), with sheer walls rising 2,000ft (600m) from the valley floor.

Before the Europeans landed in Hawaii, the valley supported a population of 10,000, who fished off its shores and grew taro inland. Many Hawaiian chiefs were raised here, including Kamehameha the Great, giving it the nickname 'Valley of the Kings'. Although the population declined greatly in the 19th century, settlement in Waipi`o continued until the 1946 tsunami flushed right through the valley, devastating everything in its path. If the overlook view isn't enough for you, head back to the little town of **Kukuihaele**, where several operators offer tours down to the valley in vans, covered wagons or on horseback.

Waipi`o Valley, childhood home of Kamehameha the Great

Hawaii and the West

Although Hawaiians lived undisturbed in their traditional manner for thousands of years, two centuries ago the first Westerners arrived, unwittingly laying a course that would irrevocably change Hawaii's fate. The islands' modern history thus began in 1778, when English explorer James Cook became the first recorded European to land there, stepping ashore on Kauai. Although Cook was killed a year later, word got out about these lush islands, located so strategically in the middle of the Pacific, and more and more Western traders began using Hawaii as a port of call.

A statue to Captain Cook at Waimea, Kauai, where he first came ashore

Young Kamehameha, still just a chief on the Big Island, fully understood the power of advanced Western technology, and his conquest of the other islands was achievable in large part from having ships and cannons obtained from the traders, and military advice from white men such as John Young (*see p68*).

After Kamehameha's death in 1819, the traditional religion was dismantled by Kamehameha II and Queen Ka`ahumanu (*see p88*), putting Hawaii into a spiritual limbo. Only a few months later, the first Christian missionaries arrived and were allowed to remain in the islands, partly due to John Young's advice. They soon created a Hawaiian alphabet and began teaching Hawaiians to read and write using a specially translated Bible. The same year, whaling ships began using Hawaii as a supply port for long hunting trips, and a new economy of growing foreign crops and livestock (leading to the import of Hispanic cowboys, or *paniolos*) to provision the ships sprang up in response.

In 1825, Ka`ahumanu herself converted to Christianity and her subjects soon followed suit. As the missionaries' influence with the government grew, so did their political power, and that of other fortune-seekers from abroad. By 1844, Kamehameha III had over two dozen white advisors, three of them his top ministers. His Great *Mahele* ('land division') of 1848 introduced private land ownership to Hawaii, where formerly chiefs held all lands in trust for the people to farm. Within a few years, whole swaths of the islands were owned by white plantation owners (many descended from missionaries), forcing the commoners into a choice between harsh servitude or unemployment. Imported labourers from China, Portugal, Korea, Japan and the Philippines began to replace the native population, which started to shrink further from lack of immunity to foreign illnesses such as smallpox, measles and Hansen's disease (leprosy).

The next half-century saw Hawaii's increasing importance as a top producer of sugar and other crops for American markets, and powerful white businessmen had a greater say in internal policy, forcing Hawaiian kings to sign a treaty abolishing trade tariffs with the US, and to approve the infamous 'Bayonet Constitution' of 1887, which relinquished much of the Crown's power to the legislature (dominated by white property

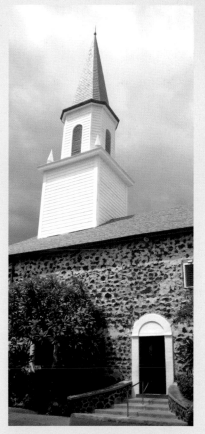

Moku`aikaua Church, built by Hawaii's first missionaries in Kailua, the Big Island

owners). When newly crowned Queen Lili`uokalani tried to regain control, they swiftly deposed her and formed their own Republic of Hawaii. Within a few years, it was officially annexed as a US territory – the final 'consummation' (in US President McKinley's words) of the brief and volatile association between Hawaii and the West.

Maui

Named after the Polynesian demigod who pulled the Hawaiian islands out of the sea using his giant fishhook, Maui is considered by beach-lovers everywhere to be synonymous with 'fun in the sun', making it Hawaii's second most popular island. Apart from fine weather and calm waters, however, there's plenty more here to captivate the imagination, including migrating humpback whales, grassy upcountry cattle ranches, the dramatic northeast-coast scenic drive, and the otherworldly volcanic landscape that lies above the clouds. Like the other islands, Maui is explored most easily by car.

Orientation

The second-largest Hawaiian island, Maui consists of two volcanoes and the flat, central isthmus between them; once it formed one giant island with Molokai, Lanai and Kaho`olawe, but rising seas turned low valleys into ocean channels. Highway 30 runs from central Kahului, the commercial centre of Maui, around the base of the West Maui Mountains to several beach resorts and the busy tourist town Lahaina. Highway 31 leads to the dry southern coast and its safe beaches, while surfers and windsurfers take Highway 36 to the breezy north coast

Maui is known for its beautiful beaches

near Pa`ia; beyond it, the notoriously twisty Hana Highway leads to the east coast. Highway 37 leads up the fertile southwestern slopes of Haleakala (10,023ft/3,055m), the massive, dormant volcano that comprises the entire eastern section of the island.

History

Polynesians from the Marquesas Islands first settled Maui around the 4th century CE. Squabbling tribal settlements were scattered around the island, with the largest population centres around Hana and Lahaina. Pi`ilani became the first chief to rule all of Maui, around the 15th century, and soon expanded his rule to Molokai,

Lanai and Kaho`olawe. Maui was ultimately defeated by his Big Island nemesis Kamehameha.

Lahaina was the royal capital in the early 1800s, and became a focus for both staid Christian missionaries and raucous Pacific whalers. After the government moved to Honolulu and the whaling industry dwindled, American and European entrepreneurs developed agriculture on Maui, devising irrigation channels to redirect rain from the east for pineapple and sugar plantations. Like the other islands, Maui has been reinvented for tourism since the decline of the plantations, although Maui still has one of Hawaii's two working sugar mills.

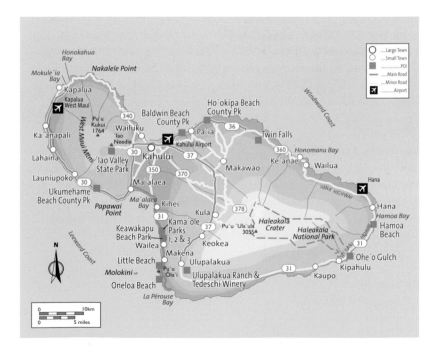

`Iao Needle, `Iao Valley State Park

THE WEST SIDE

Highway 30 runs from the central Kahului–Wailuku area around the base of the West Maui Mountains, past busy Lahaina and several beach resorts. After Nakalele Point, the road narrows and twists around cliffs and valleys, offering a long, beautiful, occasionally hair-raising coastal drive.

`Iao Valley State Park

`Iao Valley Road leads north from Wailuku to this damp windward valley. A large rock pinnacle called `**Iao Needle** stands 2,250ft (686m) tall over the `Iao Stream, which winds around a small re-creation of a Hawaiian village.

Ka`anapali

Ka`anapali was built in the 1960s alongside a stunning, 3-mile (5-km) white-sand beach. It has almost a dozen hotels and condominium resorts, two golf courses and **Whaler's Village**, a large shopping centre and a small whaling museum. Ka`anapali's beach is bisected by the cinder cone **Pu`u Keka`a** ('Black Rock'), which has terrific snorkelling around its base. The historic **Lahaina Ka`anapali & Pacific Railroad** (*www.sugarcanetrain.com*) offers scenic train rides to and from Lahaina.

Kahului

The largest town on Maui has the island's main airport and its largest shopping centres, as well as the highly regarded **Maui Arts and Cultural Center**. The **Alexander & Baldwin Sugar Museum** offers a comprehensive history of sugar-cane production on Maui. *Sugar Museum. 3957 Hansen Rd (at Hwy 350). Tel: (808) 871-8058. Open: Mon–Sat 9.30am–4pm. Closed: Sun, New Year, Thanksgiving, Christmas. Admission charge.*

Kapalua

Kapalua has hotels and condos, top-notch golf courses, and little scalloped bays with beautiful beaches and safe swimming, particularly at **Napili Bay**, **Kapalua Beach**, **Honolua Bay** and **Mokule`ia Bay**. The latter three also offer great snorkelling on offshore reefs.

Lahaina

The largest town on the west side, Lahaina was once both the Pacific

WHALE WATCHING

Late November to mid-April is the best season to see majestic Pacific humpback whales, who migrate south to breed in the warm waters around Hawaii. The best place to spot them is in the shallow channels between Maui, Lanai and Molokai. Both Lahaina and Ma`alaea Harbor feature numerous tour companies offering whale-watching trips. Reputable operators will adhere to federal laws requiring all boats to keep a safe distance from the whales.

whaling industry's main port and the capital of the Kingdom of Hawaii. Today it's a bustling, seaside tourist centre that still manages to retain some nautical charm. Many boating operators leave from its harbour, and downtown Front Street makes for an extremely pleasant stroll (*see pp78–9*). To the south are some beach parks with

good swimming and surfing, including **Launiupoko Beach Park** and **Ukemehame Beach Park**. The roadside lookout at **Papawai Point**, just north of Ma`alaea Harbor, is a great place to see whales offshore (*see text box*).

Wailuku

Wailuku has a small downtown with some classic old buildings, such as the restored `**Iao Theater**, home to a musical-theatre company, and Maui's best historical museum, the **Bailey House Museum**, a former mission house with a large collection of artefacts from life in 19th-century Maui.

Bailey House Museum. 2375A Main St. Tel: (808) 244-3326. Open: Mon–Sat 10am–4pm. Closed: Sun, New Year, Thanksgiving, Christmas. Admission charge.

Launiupoko Beach Park

Walk: Historical Lahaina

This short harbourside walk covers some of the historical highlights of downtown Lahaina, once both Hawaii's pre-eminent whaling town as well as Hawaii's royal capital from 1820 to 1845. There are also plenty of shops and restaurants to browse through on your way.

Around ¾ mile (1km). Allow 1–2 hours.

Start at the Hale Pa`ahao, located at the corner of Prison Street and Waine`e Street.

1 Hale Pa`ahao
Hawaiian for 'Stuck-in-irons House', Hale Pa`ahao prison was built in 1852 with coral rocks taken from the town's demolished fort. Both Hawaiians and foreign whalers or missionaries could end up here for any number of crimes, including public intoxication, working on the Sabbath or deserting their ship. *Open: Mon–Sat 10am–4pm. Closed: Sun. Free admission. Continue southwest along Prison Street. Turn right at Front Street and walk one block.*

2 Banyan Tree Square
The spectacular banyan tree that fills this main square was planted on 24 April 1873 on the 50th anniversary of Lahaina's first Christian mission. Today more than 20 trunks emanate in all directions. Besides being a National Historic Landmark, it's a lovely spot to sit for a while and people-watch. *Behind the tree to the southwest is the Old Courthouse.*

3 Old Lahaina Courthouse
This municipal building was constructed in 1859 to hold the governor's office, customs house, courtroom and post office. Today it has a visitors' centre with a large gift shop, an art gallery with free local exhibitions (*open: 9am–5pm*) and the **Lahaina Heritage Center** (*open: 10am–4pm; donation requested*), with historical exhibits. This site also used to be the location of the town fort; corner reconstructions of the coral-rock wall can be seen just outside the Courthouse. *Turn right on Wharf Street and walk one block north.*

4 Pioneer Inn
This hotel was built in 1901 by a Canadian mountie who pursued a suspect all the way to Maui (in vain), fell in love with a Hawaiian woman, and stayed. Some period details remain in the lobby area. *Walk northeast to Front Street and turn left.*

5 Baldwin House

This former missionary home is the oldest building in Lahaina, dating from 1834. The ground floor comprises a museum of period life, with original *koa*-wood furniture and family items. *Tel: (808) 661-3262. Open: 10am–4pm. Closed: New Year, Christmas. Admission charge. Continue up Front Street.*

6 Wo Hing Temple

Built in 1912, this two-storey building once housed a temple and meeting rooms for a mutual aid society for Chinese immigrants, and today houses an interesting little museum with displays and artefacts from the history of the Chinese in Hawaii. The outdoor cookhouse features a loop of silent film footage of local ranch life, shot by Thomas Edison in 1898. *Tel: (808) 661-5553. Open: 10am–4pm. Closed: New Year, Christmas. Admission charge.*

Walk: Historical Lahaina

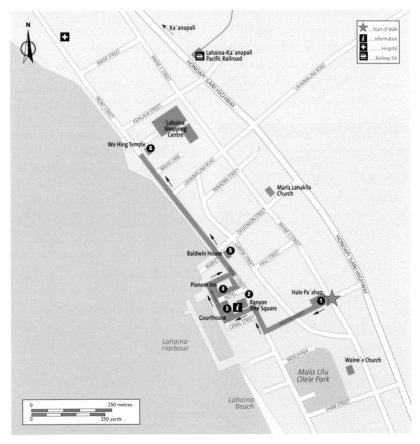

Agriculture in Hawaii

Temperate weather and rich soils have always made Hawaii a particularly fertile place for farming, although most of its crops, surprisingly, are relatively recent imports. Many plants stereotypically considered 'Hawaiian' were actually brought over in the last thousand years or so by the original Polynesian settlers, who provisioned their canoes with staple crops like *kalo* (taro), *`uala* (sweet potato), *ulu* (breadfruit), *ko* (sugar cane), *mai`a* (banana) and *niu* (coconut). For much of ancient Hawaiian history, large windward valleys like Waipi`o on the Big Island or Halawa on Molokai supported settlements of several thousand people through a combination of carefully farmed crops, livestock management and local fishing.

Captain Cook was the first Westerner on record to trade for food and supplies in Hawaii, and before long other ships began to call in during voyages around the Pacific. New crops were eventually introduced to cater for this market, including pineapples, coffee and potatoes. The massive influx of gold-seekers to California in 1849–51 boosted Hawaii's agricultural economy even more, and onions, pumpkins and oranges were exported along with the others to feed the burgeoning population of the American West.

Although sugar cane had been in Hawaii for centuries, it wasn't until the first successful sugar plantation was founded on Kauai in 1835 – possible only through the construction of a 10-mile (16-km) irrigation ditch – that 'King Cane' became a commercially viable crop. During the American Civil War (1861–5), Northerners were unable to get sugar from their usual Southern suppliers

Taro is the staple plant of Hawaii

Hawaii is famous for tropical fruits like pineapple, papaya, mango and bananas

was outstripped by imported Asian labourers, taro fields were converted to rice paddies to feed them, making rice the second-largest crop in the kingdom. During this time, the directors of the five largest agribusinesses (the 'Big Five') consolidated their powerful grip on Hawaii, taking over the government in 1893. They essentially ran Hawaii as an oligarchy until the mid-20th century, when organised labour unions, admission to US statehood and undercutting from cheaper foreign markets led to the decline and eventual closure of almost all of Hawaii's large plantations and processing companies.

Today only two sugar plantations remain in operation, and commercial Hawaiian agriculture has survived mainly through diversification. Almost half of the world's macadamia nuts come from Hawaii, and the several million pounds of Kona coffee produced annually account for most of the top end of the world's premium coffees market. Almost 5,500 farms grow around 40 crops, including ginger, tropical fruits like bananas and papayas, flowers, garden vegetables and nursery products, although with the past few decades' transformation to a tourism-based economy, agricultural revenues now account for only 1 per cent of Hawaii's GDP.

and turned instead to Hawaiian sugar, leading to an even bigger economic boom. A decade later, the pro-American King David Kalakaua signed the Reciprocity Treaty of 1875, abolishing trade tariffs between the two nations and making the Hawaiian economy almost entirely dependent on its agricultural exports.

Subsequent decades saw Americans and Europeans building more plantations around the islands and developing other commercial crops like macadamia nuts and pineapples. (At one point the island of Lanai was the world's largest pineapple plantation.) As the native population

THE SOUTH COAST

Maui's leeward shore is famed for dry, sunny weather and a long string of beaches with the island's best swimming, snorkelling, scuba diving and kayaking. Unfortunately, the area is also one of Maui's most developed. **Kihei** is a long, somewhat mundane sprawl of mid-range condos, hotels and shopping centres. Further south are the upscale areas of **Wailea** and **Makena**, featuring luxury hotels, gated communities, manicured golf courses and high-end shops.

Beaches

In Kihei, the most popular beach is the three-sectioned **Kama`ole Beach County Park**; the northern end of #1 has good snorkelling, or head to #3 for shaded picnic tables and good boogie-

The rocky shore at La Pérouse Bay

boarding. **Keawakapu Beach Park**, a little further south, is also a worthy alternative. From Wailea on, a succession of small, scalloped bays offers beautiful white-sand beaches with safe swimming. Access paths are *makai* (oceanward) from the coast road. Try **Ulua Beach** (next to the Renaissance Wailea) for boogie-boarding, or **Polo Beach** (just south of the Kea Lani Hotel) for swimming. Walk south along the sand for ten minutes to get to **Palauea Beach**, a much quieter spot with good snorkelling and boogie-boarding.

Big Beach (Oneloa Beach)

Many consider Oneloa ('long sands') – universally known as Big Beach – to be Maui's most picturesque, and indeed this broad, ½-mile (0.8-km) stretch of sand just south of **Pu`u `Ola`i**, an ancient cinder cone, is worth a visit just for its views of Kaho`olawe. Boogie-boarders love the lively surf, although offshore currents can be dangerous; there are no lifeguards, so swim with caution. Snorkellers like the calmer waters at the northern end. A path over Pu`u `Ola`i to the other side leads to **Little Beach**, a shadier and even more idyllic spot, with views of Lanai, west Maui and little Molokini Crater. It's also a popular (though illegal) nudist beach, so don't be surprised if you see some skin.

La Pérouse Bay

Three miles (5km) south of Big Beach – past fields of jagged lava from

Big Beach is one of Maui's most popular beaches

Haleakala's last eruption, in 1790 – the road ends at this rocky bit of coastline, where a bronze plaque commemorates the French explorer Jean-François de Galaup, Comte de la Pérouse, who spent three hours ashore here on 30 May 1786, becoming the first European to set foot on Maui. Although under royal orders to claim the land for France, he refused to do so out of respect for its inhabitants, and sailed off. Two years later, both his ships were lost in the Solomon Islands with no survivors.

Maui Ocean Center

A variety of exhibits is ranged around an open-air park, where you can see tropical-reef fish, seahorses, jellyfish, sharks and sea turtles, as well as displays on humpback whales and traditional Hawaiian ocean culture. *192 Ma`alaea Rd, Ma`alaea. Tel: (808) 270-7000. www.mauioceancenter.com. Open: 9am–5pm, 9am–6pm July–Aug. Admission charge.*

Molokini Crater

This mostly submerged volcano crater just 3 miles (5km) off Maui's south coast has an underwater reef full of tropical fish, making it one of Hawaii's most popular snorkelling spots. Numerous operators offer tours there from Ma`alaea Harbor or Lahaina.

THE NORTH COAST AND UPCOUNTRY

The north coast of Maui, known for its windsurfing and quaint towns, is the gateway to both the fertile mountain slopes of 'upcountry' Maui and the spectacularly scenic road to Hana (*see p90*).

Ali`i Kula Lavender Farm

Dozens of varieties of lavender and protea grow at this farm high up the southwestern slopes of Haleakala, and the gift store offers an astounding 75 different products, including body lotions, cosmetics, culinary delights like lavender honey or lavender-chocolate brownies, soaps, candles and other gifts. The farm offers several different tours, including a very popular luncheon tour that includes high tea, lunch and a cooking demonstration.

1100 Waipoli Rd, Kula. Tel: (808) 878-3004. www.aliikulalavender.com.
Gift store open: 9am–4pm.
Tours by reservation only.

Haleakala

This unmissable national park is discussed in 'Getting away from it all' (*see p122*).

Surfers head out to catch some waves at Ho`okipa Beach

Ho`okipa Beach Park

Two miles (3km) east of Pa`ia, this beach gets top honours as the best windsurfing site in Maui (and perhaps the world), although, by mutual agreement, surfers get the waves before 11am. The waters here are far too strong for non-experts, and the beach itself is not particularly fine, but the roadside lookout to its east offers a great spot for watching or photographing the action.

Makawao

A *paniolo* (cowboy) town since the 19th century, in recent years this upcountry spot has been reborn as a community for local artists, supported by the **Hui No'eau Visual Arts Center** (*2841 Baldwin Ave, Makawao; tel: (808) 572-6560; www.huinoeau.com*), which offers classes and exhibits at a stately mansion outside town. Makawao's charming main street offers rustic, false wooden storefronts with several fine cafés and restaurants, art galleries and gift shops, as well as a glass-blowing store where you can see demonstrations daily. If you're visiting in early July, don't miss the annual rodeo.

Pa`ia

This former sugar-mill town is now a colourful, bohemian enclave for New-Agers and beach bums. Its compact downtown has some of the area's best restaurants and cafés and a coterie of shops, although local accommodation is limited to a handful of B&Bs.

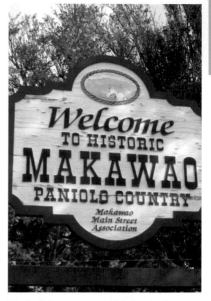

Maui still has a strong *paniolo* (cowboy) connection

Windsurfers love its proximity to famed Ho`okipa Beach, but the best swimming and bodysurfing nearby is at **Baldwin Beach Park**, 1 mile (1.6km) west of downtown.

Twin Falls

Almost 12 miles (19km) east of Pa`ia on the Hana Highway, just before the town of Huelo, a makeshift car park and food stand on the right signals the short trail leading to these two small waterfalls, the first of which has a large pool that makes a fine swimming hole. More daring folk jump from the top ledge, although there's a rope swing at the base that's just as fun. Car break-ins are common here, so don't leave valuables behind.

Drive: Upcountry Maui

This drive through the rolling green meadows of Haleakala's southwestern slopes stops at some historic and botanical sites and quaint towns. You can visit Haleakala (see p122) on the return trip, but even a cursory trip to the summit and back takes about three hours.

48 miles (77km). Allow half a day, or a full day including Haleakala.

Start at the top of Highway 37. Drive 13 miles (21km) to the left-hand turn for Holy Ghost Church.

1 Holy Ghost Church

This unusual, octagonal Portuguese Catholic church was built in 1894. The tropical baroque interior features pink walls, colourfully painted Stations of the Cross and a hand-carved gilt altar shipped from Austria. The car park offers amazing views of central Maui.
Continue south on Highway 37 for about 5 miles (8km).

2 Keokea

The row of antique green-clapboard storefronts on the right is the main street of Keokea, formerly a 19th-century Chinese migrant village. There's an art gallery and the extremely cute **Grandma's Coffee House** (*tel: (808) 878-2140; open: 6.30am–5pm*). *Drive on for 2 miles (3km).*

3 Dr Sun Yat-sen Memorial Park

The small park is dedicated to a Chinese statesman whose family once lived nearby. Incredible southern views include the leeward coast, Molokini Crater and Lanai.
Continue south for about 3 miles (5km).

4 Ulupalakua Ranch and Tedeschi Winery

Formerly a sugar mill and now a working cattle farm, Ulupalakua Ranch occupies 20,000 acres (8,094 hectares) of this grassy countryside. Carnivores and cowboy lovers should stop at the Ranch Store (*tel: (808) 878-2561; www.ulupalakuaranch.com; open: 9.30am–5pm, grill 11am–2pm*) for fresh-grilled elk burgers or country-themed gifts and souvenirs.

Maui's only winery (*tel: (877) 878-6058; www.mauiwine.com; open: 9am–5pm*) is also here; its tasting room was a cottage built for King David Kalakaua, a frequent guest of the ranch. They offer free tours of the lovely grounds and tastings of their wines.
Head back north on Highway 37 for about 8 miles (13km) and turn right

onto Highway 377 (Kekaulike Ave). Drive north for a few miles.

5 Kula Botanical Gardens

Six acres (2.4 hectares) of native tropical plants and flowers. Most is wheelchair-accessible.
Tel: (808) 878-1715. Open: 9am–4pm. Admission charge. Continue north on Highway 377. The entrance to Haleakala is about 2 miles (3km) on. Otherwise continue for another 6 miles (10km),

almost to the Highway 37 intersection, and bear right onto Hanamu Rd. At the T-junction, turn left onto Olinda Rd and continue on to Makawao.

6 Makawao

This *paniolo* town (*see p85*) has interesting shops and some fine restaurants perfect for a post-trip meal.
Continue north along Baldwin Ave (Highway 390) from Makawao through Pa`ia to return to Highway 36.

Drive: Upcountry Maui

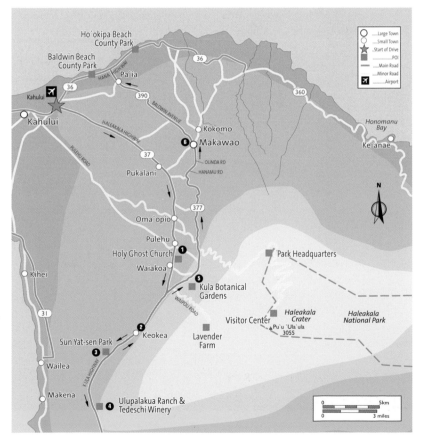

THE EAST

Although remote and sparsely populated today, the east coast of Maui once had a large Hawaiian settlement around Hana (*see p91*). While most people take the Hana Highway round-trip just for its scenic views, those wanting to get away from the touristy areas of the south and west would do well to tarry here a while to explore the uncrowded eastern coast, with its views of Mauna Kea on the Big Island across the channel on clear days.

At the time of writing, Highway 31 is closed between Kipahulu and Kaupo

HAWAII'S GREATEST QUEEN

Few affected Hawaiian history like Ka'ahumanu, Kamehameha I's favourite wife, born at Hana in 1777. Of higher birth than her husband, and just as strong-willed, upon his death she proclaimed herself queen regent, managing the kingdom for both Kamehamehas II and III (*see pp16–17*). She wrested power from the priesthood and ended the ancient *kapu* laws, and prevented Kauai's secession by kidnapping and marrying both its chief and his son. Permitting Hawaii's first missionaries to stay, she converted to Christianity in 1825 after they nursed her through a long illness. Under her proselytising, all of Hawaii had converted by her death in 1832.

The beach at Hamoa Bay

due to earthquake damage sustained in 2006, with no set plans for reopening.

Hamoa Bay

This little bay is considered by many to have one of Maui's prettiest beaches, a crescent of white sand used by Hotel Hana-Maui for its ocean-front activities. Because there are no reefs offshore, swimming and bodysurfing are safest in summer and early autumn – do not swim if the surf is high. The beach is located a few miles south of Hana, down the loop of Haneo'o Road.

'Ohe'o Gulch

Ten miles (16km) beyond Hana, a large stream runs down a long, rock 'staircase' to create these beautiful pools that tumble down to the sea. You can get a view from the highway bridge that passes above, but entering the park will let you take the easy ½-mile (0.8km) trail down to the base of the pools, or the 4-mile (6.5km) round-trip hike along the Pipiwai Trail that leads past the 200-ft (61-m) **Makahiku Falls**, through an old bamboo forest and to the 400-ft (122-m) **Waimoku Falls**.

'Ohe'o Gulch is part of Haleakala National Park, so the same admission fee will cover a visit here and to Haleakala Crater if you visit both within three days. Although the water here is tempting, it is extremely dangerous to swim in the pools or jump from the waterfalls, and several adults and children have died here in

The pools of 'Ohe'o Gulch

recent years doing just that.
Open: 24 hours. Admission charge.

Palapala Ho'omau Church

This unassuming, whitewash-and-green-timber church, built in 1857 amid some lovely clifftop gardens near the **Kipahulu Point Park**, is the site of **Charles Lindbergh's grave**. The famed Atlantic aviator retired to Maui near the end of his life and died nearby in 1974. If the road beyond Kipahulu has been reopened, take the ocean-side turn ¼ mile (0.5km) after mile marker 41, then turn left onto the dirt road leading through the trees.

Drive: Hana Highway

This narrow highway, comprising highways 31, 36 and 360, and constructed in 1926, offers some of Hawaii's most spectacular coastal scenery – and notorious driving conditions – as it winds over one-lane bridges, around cliffside corners and past countless waterfalls.

A 70-mile (112km) round-trip. Allow a full day, leaving as early as possible – the outbound drive can take 4–5 hours with stops. Buy supplies and fill your tank in Pa`ia; the only other service station is in Hana, where most businesses close around dusk.

Begin at mile marker 0 on Highway 360, about 9½ miles (15km) east of Pa`ia.

1 Waikamoi Ridge Trail

The rest stop between mile markers 9 and 10 offers a picnic area and a 1-mile (1.5-km) loop trail up the (sometimes muddy) Waikamoi Ridge, past eucalyptus, *hala* trees and tall stalks of bamboo, to a grassy clearing with another picnic shelter. A little further down the road, a wide spot just before a hairpin turn offers limited parking for the **Waikamoi Falls**, where a steep trail leads down to the pool at its base.

2 Honomanu Bay

After mile marker 13, the road drops down to sea level, offering lovely views of the black gravel beach at the mouth of the lush Honomanu Valley. It's popular with local surfers, but swimming here is not advisable.

3 Ke`anae

Just before the 17-mile marker, the gardens of the **Ke`anae Arboretum** (*open: dawn–dusk; free admission*) offer trails through the tropical flora of this lush, tapered valley, including taro fields and rainforest. The **Ke`anae Peninsula**, down to the left just after the Arboretum, leads to a small Hawaiian village with a picturesque rocky-coastline setting. Back on the highway, the 'Halfway to Hana' food stand (*open: 8.30am–4pm*) past mile marker 18 offers food and smoothies.

If it's late in the day, consider turning around here to avoid driving back from Hana in the dark.

4 Wailua

Several roadside lookouts about 1 mile (1.5km) past Ke`anae offer views of another Hawaiian village at Wailua Bay. The **Wailua Valley State Wayside** on your right has only a few spots for cars, but the ridge platform up the stairs has a fantastic vantage of the coast as well as inland over Wailua Valley. Continue slowly around the next bend so you don't rush by the gorgeous waterfall at the one-lane bridge.

5 Wai`anapanapa State Park

Don't miss this coastal state park just before Hana, where a black-sand beach surrounded by volcanic rocks, natural blowholes and a cavernous lava tube offers fantastic opportunities for exploration and photography. Several marked hiking trails follow the striking coastline, including one that leads southeast to the ruins of the **Ohala Heiau**.

6 Hana

This tiny town is home to a cattle ranch, a luxury hotel, a handful of B&Bs, and a few shops and restaurants, including the charmingly small-town **Hasegawa's General Store**, a good place to pick up supplies for the return trip. Keawa Place leads down to **Hana Beach**, the safest swimming in the area. A short trail leads around its headland to a plaque marking the birthplace of the great Queen Ka`ahumanu (*see p88*).

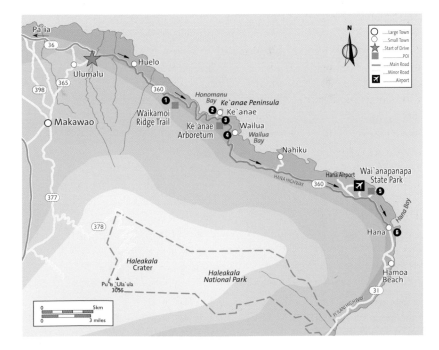

Kauai

Don't feel sorry for Kauai. Although it's the oldest, smallest, least populated, and the most remote of Hawaii's four main islands, it's universally regarded – with much truth – as the most beautiful. There's no denying that 'The Garden Isle' lives up to its name, with pristine wilderness painted with infinite shades of green, lofty waterfalls spilling from jagged mountain ridges, and a rippling chain of serrated seacliffs. At the other extreme, the grooved walls of the ancient, river-carved canyon on the leeward side are a compelling study in reds and browns.

Kauai's development is confined to the coastlines, leaving an amazing 95 per cent of the interior untouched and inaccessible by any land vehicle. If you take one helicopter ride in your life, this is the place to do it.

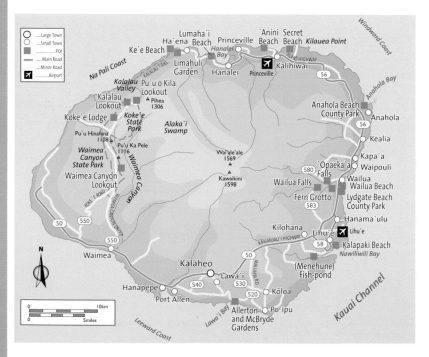

A helicopter tour is the best way to see Kauai's amazing scenery

Orientation

Kauai forms a roughly elliptical shape around the central peaks of Kawaikini (5,243ft/1,598m) and the slightly shorter Mount Wai`ale`ale, one of the wettest spots on earth, averaging 460in (11,680mm) of rain annually. With an area of only 552sq miles (1,430sq km), no point on the island is more than 12 miles (19km) from the ocean. To the west is the Waimea Canyon and Koke`e State Park; to the northwest is the large, boggy Alaka`i Swamp and the sheer, stunning seacliffs of the Na Pali coast. Much of the far west coast is occupied by the US Navy's Pacific Missile Range Facility, the largest of its kind in the world.

History

Separated from the other islands by the deep channel that bears its name, Kauai is thought to have been settled by a different, earlier wave of Polynesians from the others. Its distance ensured independence – Kauai and its tiny neighbour Ni`ihau (*see pp108–9*) were the only islands Kamehameha the Great never conquered. Kauai's great chief Kaumuali`i finally ceded peacefully in 1810 to avoid further bloodshed and became the island's governor.

Kauai also saw Europe's first recorded contact with Hawaii when Captain Cook landed at Waimea on 19 January 1778. Hawaii's first sugar plantation was started here in 1835. Today its sugar mill is one of only two in operation in Hawaii (the other is in Maui).

In 1992, Hurricane Iniki – the strongest ever to hit Hawaii – damaged almost three-quarters of the homes on Kauai and killed three people.

THE EAST SIDE
Beaches

A long string of beaches runs along the east coast, although the winds and lack of an offshore reef make many of them too exposed for safe swimming.

Anahola Beach County Park

About 5½ miles (9km) north of Kapa`a, turn *makai* (oceanward) onto Aliomanu Road (after mile marker 13) to get to this sweeping beach with safe swimming protected by Kahala Point.

Kalapaki Beach

Just beyond the Anchor Cove Shopping Center in Lihu`e, this beach is tucked away in a safe little pocket of Nawiliwili Bay. It's a good place for beginner surfers, too.

Sheltered swimming at Lydgate State Park Beach

Lydgate State Park

Just north of Lihu`e behind the Aloha Beach Resort, this beach has two large protected lagoons, great for snorkelling and family swimming.

Wailua Beach

Boogie-boarders and surfers love the high waves at this beach, just north of the mouth of the Wailua River.

Kapa`a

In the wooden storefronts of downtown Kapa`a you'll find the atmosphere of an old Hawaiian plantation town, as well as your best food options on the east side. The little triangle of streets holds a panoply of galleries, gift shops, cafés and restaurants, including one recently voted 'Best Restaurant on Kauai' (*see p169*). Just up the road, a Farmer's Market sells produce, handmade

---

HELICOPTER TOURS

The best (and only) way to see most of Kauai's stunning scenery is by helicopter. Reputable companies with excellent safety records make daily trips from Lihue`e, Port Allen and Princeville.

Air Kauai (Lihu`e) *Tel: (800) 972-4666.*
www.airkauai.com
Heli USA (Princeville) *Tel: (866) 966-1234.*
www.heliusa.com
Inter-Island (Port Allen) *Tel: (800) 656-5009.*
www.interislandhelicopters.com
Island (Lihu`e) *Tel: (800) 829-5999.*
www.islandhelicopters.com
Jack Harter (Lihu`e) *Tel: (888) 245-2001.*
www.helicopters-kauai.com
Safari (Lihu`e) *Tel: (800) 326-3356.*
www.safarihelicopters.com
Will Squyres (Lihu`e) *Tel: (888) 245-3354.*
www.willsquyres.com

cosmetics, clothing, crafts, jewellery and gifts (*open: Wed–Sun 8am–4pm*).

King's Highway

The valley of the Wailua River – the only navigable river in Hawaii – was once the seat of Kauai's greatest chiefs, including Kaumuali`i, the last ruler of Kauai. Now Highway 580, this was once a trail of royal and sacred sites, including several *heiaus*, that followed the river all the way up to Mount Wai`ale`ale. Few traces of most of the *heiaus* remain; the best-preserved one is the large **Poli`ahu Heiau** about 1 mile (1.6km) up on the left side. Surrounded by palm trees, the site also offers a lovely view over the broad Wailua River. The next overlook on the right offers a view of `**Opaeka`a Falls**, named 'rolling shrimp' after the tiny crustacea once

harvested from its pool. Across the road is the entrance for the **Kamokila Hawaiian Village**, which offers tours of a re-created Hawaiian fishing village as well as hiking and canoe trips (including to Fern Grotto). *Kamokila. Tel: (808) 823-0559. www.kamokila.com. Open: 9am–5pm. Admission charge.*

Lihu`e

The largest town on Kauai, Lihu`e isn't especially prepossessing. Once a plantation village for the nearby sugar-cane farms, it grew to its present size only after 1930, when a new airport and the dredging of Nawiliwili Harbor (now a cruise-liner port) made it the island's first stop for visitors. Besides a few historical attractions, it has some of Kauai's less expensive accommodation

Old wooden storefront in downtown Kapa`a

The Wailua River is popular for boat trips

and a central location that facilitates day trips to the north and south coasts.

Grove Farm Homestand

One of the earliest sugar plantations on the island, Grove Farm was built in 1864 by George Wilcox, son of missionaries from the north coast. Book well in advance to take a guided tour of the estate's mansion (with a beautiful *koa*-wood staircase), cottages and fruit orchard.

Nawiliwili Rd. Tel: (808) 245-3202. Tours: Mon, Wed & Thur by reservation only. Closed: public holidays. Admission charge.

Kauai Museum

This two-building museum located in the middle of Lihu`e has a permanent collection of traditional Hawaiian artefacts, many from the personal collection of the Wilcox family, as well as rotating current exhibits on Hawaiian, Polynesian and Japanese culture, and displays detailing the history and geology of Kauai.

4428 Rice St. Tel: (808) 245-6931. www.kauaimuseum.org. Open: Mon–Fri 9am–4pm, Sat 10am–4pm. Closed: Sun, New Year, 4 July, Labor Day, Thanksgiving, Christmas. Admission charge.

Kilohana Plantation

This elegant estate was built in 1935 by Gaylord Wilcox, scion of one of the island's most powerful sugar-cane families. Besides featuring an elegant restaurant, twice-weekly *lu`aus* and some upscale gifts, jewellery and clothing shops, they offer historical estate tours in either intimate carriages or larger

wagons drawn by Clydesdale horses.
*3–2087 Kaumualii Hwy. Tel: (808) 245
5608. www.kilohanakauai.com*

Menehune Fish-pond

Take Hulemalu Road west of Nawiliwili
Harbor to reach a small overlook with a
vista of this large fish-pond (*see box
p114*), created from a bend in the
Hule`ia Stream and used to raise
mullet. A legendary race of dwarfs
who settled the islands in ancient times,
the *menehune*, was supposed to have
built large constructions like these
completely overnight. Historians think
menehune comes from a Tahitian word
for 'commoner', and that over centuries
their lower social caste became
translated into tales of shorter stature.

Wailua Falls and Fern Grotto

Five miles (8km) north of Lihu`e
on Highway 583, you'll find one
of the islands' prettiest waterfalls in
the twin streams of Wailua Falls,
which often casts rainbows in the
mist as it gushes over a steep ledge to
a pool 80ft (24m) below. They gained
international fame from the opening
sequence of the 1970s–80s TV show
Fantasy Island.

Further downstream is one of Kauai's
best-known tourist attractions, the Fern
Grotto, an ancient, water-carved cave
draped with a thick canopy of hanging
ferns. The only way there is by boat; a
few local operators run trips, departing
every 30 minutes (9am–4pm) from the
south side of the river's mouth. Some
might consider the animated
commentary and Hawaiian guitar
serenades a bit kitschy, although the
daily weddings held here attest to some
sense of the romantic.
Smith's. *Tel: (808) 821-6895.
www.smithskauai.com*
Wai`ale`ale Boat Tours.
Tel: (808) 822-4908.

Wailua Falls

Kauai

THE SOUTH SHORE AND THE WEST
Allerton and McBryde Gardens

Two of Kauai's three best tropical botanic gardens are set among 200 acres (81 hectares) of the remote Lawa`i Valley. (The third is the Limahuli Garden, see p104). The land, once the retreat of Queen Emma, was later bought by a Chicago banker who, with his architect son, transformed the valley's *makai* side into a collection of aesthetically designed 'rooms', filled with European-inspired fountains and pools, gazebos and statuary surrounded by tropical plants from all over the world, such as heliconia, frangipani and the rippled-root Moreton Bay fig tree.

Wild chickens roam free all around Kauai

Allerton Garden can be seen only by guided tour, which must be booked in advance. Further back is the McBryde Garden, viewable by self-guided tour, which has more of an emphasis on conservation – its collection of native and endemic Hawaiian plants is the largest in the world, including the *Brighamia insignis* bellflower, of which only one specimen exists in the wild.

Transport to both gardens is provided from the Visitor Center.

National Tropical Botanical Garden
4425 Lawa`i Rd, Koloa. Tel: (808) 742-2623. Visitor Center open: 8.30am–5pm. Allerton Garden tours (reservations required; no children under 10): Mon–Sat 9am, 10am, 1pm & 2pm, call for Sun times. McBryde Garden tram: 9.30am–2.30pm (leaves hourly). Admission charge.

Hanapepe

Located near Port Allen, once Kauai's main port (since replaced by the larger Nawiliwili Harbor), this town was started by Chinese migrants who had finished their plantation work contracts and converted the old taro patches in the valley to rice paddies. The main street's wooden storefronts played the part of an Australian outback town in the TV mini-series *The Thorn Birds*, and today contain a coterie of art galleries, speciality gift shops and cafés. A 'swinging bridge' (sturdier than it sounds) offers a footpath across the river.

Waimea Canyon

Po`ipu

The southernmost point on the island, Po`ipu is Kauai's most popular beach resort, populated with resort hotels and condominiums, a string of lovely beaches (the favourite being Po`ipu Beach Park, with lifeguards and a playground) and a professional-calibre golf course (home to the PGA Grand slam since 1994). Nearby **Koloa** was the site of the first sugar plantation in Hawaii.

Waimea Canyon

Called by some 'the Grand Canyon of the Pacific', Waimea Canyon can't compare to its mainland cousin in terms of size, but certainly offers some spectacular scenery. A massive, 10-mile-long (16km) gorge that's over 3,000ft (915m) deep in places, the canyon was originally formed by plate movements that once nearly split the island in two, and then carved even further by the Waimea River. The striped ridges offer an infinite palette of rust-reds, cinnamons, ochres and burnt umbers overlaid with emerald and jade-green foliage. Several lookouts line Waimea Canyon Drive as it climbs the ridge to Koke`e State Park (*see pp122–3*), where more lookouts are set above the Na Pali coast. At the base of the canyon is the town of **Waimea**, the site of Captain Cook's first landing in Hawaii. The main square has a statue of the explorer and some shops and restaurants.

Traditional Hawaiian life

Ancient Hawaiians relied on an oral history, sung as chants and passed down over thousands of years, to recount their mythology and genealogies. The first written accounts of Hawaiian history were recorded by early explorers and missionaries.

Beliefs

The four main Hawaiian gods were Kane, god of the earth, life and light; Kanaloa, god of the sea, the underworld and darkness; Lono, god of fertility, the harvest and peace; and Ku, god of warfare, the only one worshipped with human sacrifice. There were scores of lesser gods, including Pele, the volcano goddess, Laka, goddess of *hula* dancing, and the demigod Maui, son of the goddess Hina, who pulled up the Hawaiian islands from the seabed with his fishhook and caught the sun from Mt Haleakala, forcing it to slow down to grant more light during summer months.

Hawaiians also believed in the concept of *mana*, the spiritual essence inherent in all things, living or inanimate; some, like powerful rulers, had more than others. *Mana* was extremely precious and closely guarded, being increased – or lost – by great accomplishments, victory (or defeat), or use of sacred objects.

A traditional Hawaiian *hale* (house)

Society

Pre-contact Hawaii was separated into a feudal society of four castes: *ali`i* (chiefs, nobles), a ruling class structured by bloodlines and leadership abilities; *kahuna* (priests), who performed religious rites and advised the *ali`i*; the *maka`ainana*

Re-created canoes and structures at the Pu'uhonua O Honaunau place of refuge

coastal settlements for shade, food and clothing, crops like taro, sugar cane and bananas were raised in inland terraces with irrigation channels, and further up the mountain, trees were harvested for canoes and construction while basalt was quarried for tools and weapons.

Laws

The complex system of *kapu* ('laws') is believed to have been introduced by Pa'ao, a Tahitian priest from the last great wave of Polynesian settlement. Some laws conserved scarce resources; a koa tree could be cut down only if two were planted to replace it. Other laws enforced the power of the *ali'i*; it was forbidden to step on the shadow cast by a chief, since that could steal his *mana*. Many *kapu* were concerned with food; women were forbidden to prepare meals or to eat with men, so men had to cook all meals as well as use separate ovens and utensils for women's food. Additionally, women could not eat pork, certain kinds of fish, coconuts or bananas.

(commoners), responsible for all food production, construction and craft-making, who fought for the *ali'i*; and the *kauwa* (slaves), including people of the lowest birth or prisoners of war, forced to serve the *ali'i* or used as human sacrifices.

Islands were divided into wedge shapes called *ahupua'a*, from the top of the central mountain down to the coast, ensuring equal access to natural resources. Local *ali'i* owned the land in trust, apportioning it out for cultivation by the *maka'ainana*; fish were netted in shallow bays, coconut palms were planted near the

The punishment for breaking the most serious *kapu* was death, but a law-breaker could obtain clemency by chiefly fiat or by eluding pursuers to reach a *pu'uhonua* ('place of refuge'), the reward for which was full pardon (*see p55*); kings and queens were also considered living *pu'uhonuas*.

THE NORTH COAST

One of Hawaii's most beautiful coasts and home to some very exclusive real estate, the northern shore has stunning coastal views and great beaches, a lovely scenic drive (*see p106*) and the stark beauty of the ancient Na Pali cliffs.

Hanalei

The calm, crescent-shaped bay at the mouth of the Hanalei River is quite possibly the prettiest in Hawaii, with golden-sand beaches set off by palm trees and perfect views of the ruffled Na Pali Coast ridges in the distance. It's ideal for strolling, but the safest swimming is at the far-end beaches of Waikoko (*see p106*) and Pu`u Poa (*see p105*).

A CINEMATIC PARADISE

Hollywood has been drawn to Hawaii for decades, and dozens of movies and TV shows have been filmed on Kauai, with the island standing in for an Amazon rainforest (*Raiders of the Lost Ark*), an African village (*Outbreak*) and a cattle town in rural Australia (*The Thorn Birds*). Others filmed here include the *Jurassic Park* movies, the Elvis Presley musical *Blue Hawaii*, the 1976 remake of *King Kong,* and the TV show *Gilligan's Island.* The north coast's Hanalei Bay and Lumaha`i Beach were most famously used in the 1958 musical *South Pacific.* Check local bookstores for *The Kaua`i Movie Book,* a full-colour picture book detailing famous local shoots.

The little town of Hanalei is the north coast's main place for food, shops and supplies, courtesy of two shopping centres facing each other across the

The perfect crescent of Hanalei Bay

highway. The **Hanalei Center** holds restaurants and shops in an old school building, including an organic food market, a music store for ukelele fans and the irresistible Yellowfish Trading Company (*tel: (808) 826-1227*), which has a great collection of artwork, antiques and beautifully kitschy pieces of old Hawaiiana, including vintage 'aloha' shirts. The **Ching Young Village** has more restaurants and clothing and gift shops, as well as a supermarket and an equipment hire store for camping, water sports and bicycles.

Kalihiwai

Kalihiwai Road once spurred off the highway in a complete loop, until its bridge over the Kalihiwai River was washed away in a 1957 tsunami and was never reconstructed. (Highway 56 still runs over a larger bridge further upstream.) The road now exists in two separate sections, each leading to some noteworthy beaches.

The first half of the road curves to the left from a *makai* (oceanward) turn just before mile marker 24 and the main bridge. Take the first right turn onto the dirt road that ends in a small car park; a somewhat steep trail leads down to **Secret Beach**, which runs for ½ mile (0.8km) east towards Kilauea Point. The swimming is not really safe even in summer, but the cliffside setting offers a fantastic beach stroll. It's popular with locals for meditation and nude sunbathing (which is actually illegal under Hawaiian law). Or if you

The taro patches of Hanalei Valley are a national wildlife refuge

prefer, follow Kalihiwai Road around to the left and continue to the end, where the roadside **Kalihiwai Beach** offers great surfing and boogie-boarding.

Back on the highway, sneak a careful peek inland as you cross the bridge to see the wide **Kalihiwai Falls**. The first turn after the bridge leads to the second half of Kalihiwai Road; take the left fork and follow it down to reach `**Anini Beach Park**, a long beach that offers safe swimming and fantastic snorkelling on the huge coral reef about 200yds (180m) offshore, as well as one of Kauai's nicest beachside campgrounds. Sundays in summer see polo games held in the fields across the road.

Kilauea Point Lighthouse

Kilauea Point

When it was built in 1913, the lighthouse on top of Kauai's northernmost point featured the world's largest clamshell lens, although it's since been replaced by an automatic light nearby. Now this high, rocky promontory and a few surrounding islets have been set aside as a wildlife sanctuary for golden plovers, Hawaiian *nene*, frigate birds and albatrosses. With the free binocular stands you may also be able to spot monk seals and spinner dolphins. In winter months it's a prime location for humpback whales, but the striking coastal views are worthwhile year-round. Rangers lead one-hour hikes every morning, for which you need to make a reservation with **Kilauea Point National Wildlife Refuge**. On your way to the point you'll pass the small **Kong Lung Center**, featuring a cute courtyard with a bakery-café, a fine restaurant and several gift shops.

Kilauea Point National Wildlife Refuge. Off Hwy 56, Kilauea. Tel: (808) 828-1413. http://pacificislands.fws.gov. Open: Mon–Fri 10am–4pm. Closed: Sat, Sun, New Year, Thanksgiving, Christmas. Admission charge.

Limahuli Garden

The narrow Limahuli Valley was once sustainably farmed by Hawaiians, who created a series of taro-field terraces from lava rocks here almost a thousand years ago. Although Western ownership later led to decades of deforestation from cattle grazing, the valley was restored to its earlier state in the late 20th century and turned into this award-winning nature preserve. A ¾-mile (1.2-km) self-guided trail through the *makai* (oceanward) end of the valley features the taro terraces, native trees like *plumeria* and *ohi`a* and fantastic ocean views. Guided tours are also available.

5–8291 Kuhio Hwy, Ha`ena. Tel: (808) 826-1053. www.ntbg.org. Open: Tue–Sat 9.30am–4pm. Closed: Sun, Mon. Admission charge.

Na Pali Coast State Park

Discussed in 'Getting away from it all'
(*see p123*).

Princeville

Once a sugar plantation and cattle
ranch, the southern headland above
Hanalei Bay is now Kauai's most
exclusive resort area, home to luxury
hotels with perfect bay views, golf
courses, upscale condominiums, a small
shopping centre with a service station
and its own airport. There are no real
sights to speak of aside from some
lovely beaches. Don't be put off by the
imposing gate house; by state law all of
Hawaii's beaches are open to the public.
Pali Ke Kua Beach, also known as
'Hideaways', has good surfing and
snorkelling in the summer; its access
path is near the tennis courts of the
Pali Ke Kua condos on Ka Huku Road.
The bayfront **Pu`u Poa Beach**, which
runs from the Hanalei River past the
palatial Princeville Hotel, is an absolute
gem, with good swimming and
snorkelling and splendid views of the
Na Pali coast.

Kauai's mountains as seen from Princeville

Drive: Princeville to Na Pali

This drive runs the final 10 miles (16km) of the Prince Kuhio Highway (Route 560) as it winds along the north coast towards the towering Na Pali cliffs, with scenic views and picturesque beaches along the way.

Allow at least half a day if stopping for meals and beach visits.

Start at the Princeville Shopping Center (which has the only petrol station on this route) and follow the road west.

1 Hanalei Valley Lookout

Just after the shops on the left is a lookout over this curving valley at the base of Hihimanu ('beautiful') Mountain, with a patchwork of taro fields lining either side of the Hanalei River. The valley is a federal wildlife refuge dedicated to Kauai's endangered waterbirds – keep an eye out for herons, ducks or moorhens in the irrigation channels.

2 One-lane bridges

One mile (1.6km) on is the first of seven old (but sturdy) one-lane bridges. As the road winds along the coastline, you'll see undulating mountains with the occasional waterfall off to your left. After a few minutes you'll come to the town of **Hanalei** (*see pp102–3*), your last real chance for food and supplies.
Note: Local etiquette dictates that drivers allow oncoming cars to cross one-lane bridges in small groups, not alternating singly.

3 Wai`oli Hui`ia Church and Mission House

Just past Hanalei is this 1912 church, painted a deep emerald green, with stained-glass windows the colour of jade and lapis lazuli, and embellished with small knots of palm trees. Adjacent is the original hipped-roof 1841 church (now a social hall), and the 19th-century house once home to several generations of missionary families. The ground floor is open for tours.
Tel: (808) 245-3202.
Open: Tue, Thur, Sat 9am–3pm.
Closed: Mon, Wed, Fri, Sun, public holidays.
Donation requested.

4 Hanalei Bay

It's gorgeous, but the only safe swimming here is at the western end's **Waikoko Beach**, beyond the mouth of the stream that crosses **Wai`oli Beach Park**.

5 Lumaha`i Beach

This photogenic beach may be familiar from its appearance in *South Pacific*. There's a little overlook and trailhead at a wide spot before milepost 5, or you can drive a bit further down to access the beach at its western end. Although it's lovely for a romantic stroll, the waters are too dangerous for swimming.

6 Tunnels Beach

This popular beach, about 3 miles (5km) further on, is a safe spot for swimming and snorkelling. A lifeguard is posted at the western end. You may also see yachts, windsurfers and kitesurfers. Access the beach from the short dirt road that serves as a car park, or continue on to **Ha`ena Beach Park** and walk east along the shore.

7 Ha`ena State Park and Ke`e Beach

If you don't feel like stopping at the **Limahuli Garden** (*see p104*), continue to Ke`e Beach at the end of the road at milepost 10. Walk east through the grove of trees and look back from the beach to see the ridges of the Na Pali cliffs against the horizon. The 11-mile (18-km) Kalalau Trail (*see p123*) starts from an information kiosk off the car park.

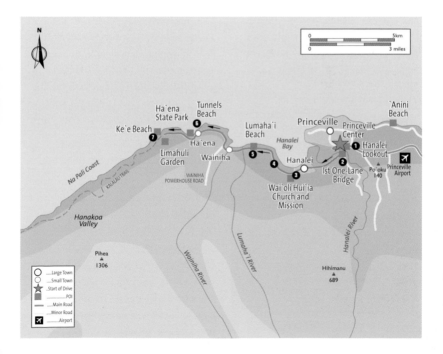

The forbidden islands

Molokai and Lanai may be the least-visited Hawaiian islands, but it's almost guaranteed that you'll never see Kaho`olawe and Ni`ihau on any travel itinerary. Here's why.

Kaho`olawe

The smallest of the eight main Hawaiian islands, Kaho`olawe comprises just 45sq miles (116sq km) around the summit of Mt Pu`u Moaulanui, which rises only 1,477ft (450m) above sea level. About 1.2 million years ago, it was part of Maui Nui ('greater Maui'), a single island formed with immediate neighbours Maui, Molokai and Lanai. By 200,000 years ago, rising seas filled in the 'saddles' between the peaks to result in four separate islands.

In the rain shadow of Maui's massive Mt Haleakala, Kaho`olawe is dry and today mostly barren, although archaeological evidence shows that Kaho`olawe once held small agricultural settlements.

Since the 19th century, Kaho`olawe has been used as everything from a short-lived penal colony to a livestock ranch. When Pearl Harbor was attacked in 1941, the US military began using it for training and firing grounds. Hawaiian protests in the 1970s eventually led to President Bush terminating live-fire training in 1990. Today the island is a reserve set aside for native Hawaiian cultural use or preservation efforts, although this is complicated by the fact that much of the island was never properly cleared of unexploded ammunition.

Ni`ihau

Many dream of owning a tropical island; in 1864, a Scottish farmer named Elizabeth Sinclair bought this one for $10,000 (around $125,000 today) from King Kamehameha V. Situated 18 miles (29km) off Kauai, Ni`ihau is still owned by her descendants, the sugar-farming Gay

The island of Ni`ihau as seen from Kauai

Twenty-Mile Beach, with west Maui and Lanai across the water

and Robinson family, who also own much of Kauai. (Sinclair soon realised that Ni`ihau, with just 12in/305mm of rain per year, was of little agricultural use.)

The people of Ni`ihau, estimated at 5,000 pre-contact, were understandably outraged at the sale of their home, and many emigrated in disgust. In 1898, the Robinsons enacted a strict policy of isolation, closing off the island to the world – even the remaining islanders had to get permission for visiting relatives. Ever since then, Ni`ihau has remained frozen in time; traditional Hawaiian culture is preserved and still practised, save for a devotion to Christianity. Even more uniquely, Ni`ihau is the only place in the world where Hawaiian is still spoken as a primary language. Because missionaries simplified Hawaiian on the other islands (the 12-letter alphabet was their invention), Ni`ihau Hawaiian is believed to be the purest and most accurately pronounced strain to exist.

Today about 200 Hawaiians live here in isolation, without airport, electricity, modern plumbing, cars or paved roads, mostly in the village of Pu`uwai ('heart'). Since Ni`ihau Ranch closed down in 1999, the residents survive on federal welfare and subsistence fishing and farming. Many also make intricate necklaces from tiny shells that wash ashore, which fetch high prices on the other islands. The only legal way for tourists to set foot on Ni`ihau is to take a high-priced helicopter tour (*www.niihau.us*) from Kauai, which lands on deserted beaches far from Pu`uwai for a few hours of swimming and snorkelling, said to be among the best in Hawaii.

Molokai and Lanai

These small islands off the coast of Maui, the fifth and sixth smallest in the chain, are the least developed in Hawaii, and the least visited, but the lack of crowds and modern development may make them the perfect holiday for some. Molokai, often called the 'most Hawaiian' island, has an unhurried, rural lifestyle, with no traffic lights and just 7,000 residents. Lanai has only one real town and about 3,000 people. There's no public transportation on either island, so hiring a car is essential.

Orientation

Molokai consists of volcanic mountain ridges to the east and west, with central plains between them. The eastern half comprises the rainforest-covered Kamakou mountain ridge and coastal settlements, including the largest town, Kaunakakai. The northern valleys west of Halawa Valley are uninhabited and all but inaccessible. To the west is the Mauna Loa ridge and a string of white-sand beaches. Jutting out from Molokai's northern coast is the flat, remote Kalaupapa Peninsula and some of the world's steepest sea cliffs, many more than 3,000ft (914m) high.

Lanai (just 104sq miles/270sq km) sits a few miles off the coasts of Molokai and Maui. In the rain shadow of Maui's Mt Haleakala, it's a rather dry, high mound of red dirt, with a low, forested mountain ridge running down the centre. Lana`i City sits in the centre of the ridge at about 1,600ft (488m) above sea level and is home to all of Lanai's businesses except for one of its

Lookout over the Halawa Valley

two luxury resorts, located on the south coast.

History

Molokai at its peak may have supported up to 30,000 inhabitants. Its large network of fish-ponds (*see p114*) made it a popular prize for ancient chiefs. It was mostly ignored by Europeans due to a lack of good harbours, but in the past century, Molokai has been home to a cattle ranch and several pineapple plantations; today a few large coffee farms operate in the northwest.

More barren than Molokai, Lanai's population never rose above a few thousand. In 1922 the land was purchased by businessman Jim Dole, who turned Lanai into the world's largest pineapple plantation. Its current owner, billionaire David Murdock, phased out pineapples in the 1990s to convert Lanai into a premium tourist destination.

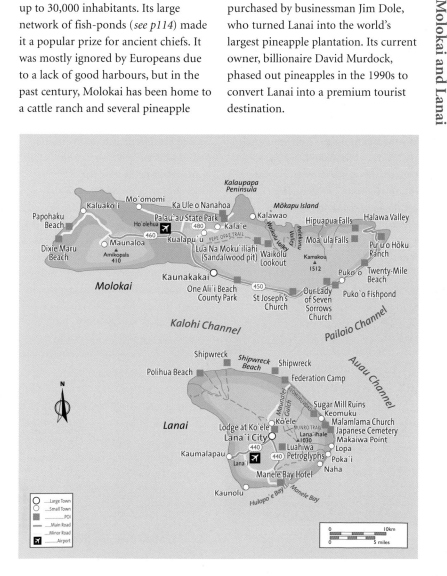

MOLOKAI AND LANAI
Molokai

Kaunakakai, Molokai's main population centre, is located in the middle of the southern coast. Most of the island's few shops, restaurants, hotels and vacation condos are located in or around this quiet little town, except for a plush resort hotel, a cinema and an engaging little kite factory and gift store to be found in the tiny former plantation town **Maunaloa**, located on the western ridge; the western coast beyond has Molokai's only real beach resort area at **Kaluako`i**. For a particularly scenic drive (*see pp116–17*), follow Highway 450 along the southeastern coast to the end of the road at Halawa Valley.

Former plantation village Maunaloa still has a rural feel

Halawa Valley

This lush, remote windward valley at the island's eastern tip was first settled by Polynesians over 1,400 years ago, and at one time was home to as many as a thousand people. Today, fewer than a dozen live here, on small farms completely off the grid. The spectacular 250-ft (75-m) Moa`ula Falls cascade down the back of the valley, reachable only by a guided hike (*see p117*).

Kalaupapa

This peninsula, once a colony for people afflicted with leprosy (*see p118*), is also a historical state park open to visitors only by guided tour, which must be booked in advance, either directly through **Damien Tours** or as part of a package with a transportation company. There are three ways to get down to Kalaupapa: a nine-minute flight from Molokai's main airport (or slightly longer ones from Honolulu or Maui); a mule ride down the 26 switchbacks of the 3-mile (5-km) cliffside trail; or hiking the trail yourself (in which case we recommend booking a flight for the return).

Kalaupapa National Historic Park
Tel: (808) 567-5802. www.nps.gov/kala

Tour/transportation companies:
Damien Tours *Tel: (808) 567-6171*
Molokai Air Shuttle *Tel: (808) 567-6847 (Molokai) or (808) 545-4988 (Oahu)*
Molokai Mule Ride *Tel: (800) 567-7550. www.muleride.com*

The remote Kalaupapa Peninsula

Pacific Wings Express *Tel: (888) 866-5022. www.pacificwings.com*
Paragon Air *Tel: (808) 244-3356. www.paragon-air.com*

Kualapu`u

Once a workers' village for the nearby sugar and pineapple plantation, this area north of Kaunakakai is now home to a large **coffee farm**; you can sample the wares at their roadside espresso bar and gift shop or take a tour of the estate. A few miles northeast of town on Highway 470 are the preserved remains of the **R W Meyer Sugar Mill**, part of the **Molokai Museum and Cultural Center**. The highway ends at **Palau`au State Park**, where you can find fantastic views from the lookout

over Kalaupapa Peninsula, or hike a short forest trail to see the aptly named **Phallic Rock**, which, according to legend, would cause young women who spent a night beneath it to fall pregnant.
Molokai Coffee Company. Tel: (808) 487-9600. www.molokaicoffee.com
Molokai Museum. Tel: (808) 567-6436. Open: Mon–Sat 10am–2pm. Closed: Sun, public holidays. Admission charge.

Western beaches

Molokai's west coast has some beautiful beaches, but most are too exposed to make them good for swimming.
Papohaku Beach is an impressively broad white-sand beach with pounding surf that makes it ideal for long walks

Remains of a fish-pond wall on the coast of Molokai

and sunset watching, as long as you stay on dry land. Safer swimming can be found at **Kepuhi Beach** – in summer if the waters are calm – and at the small, enclosed lagoon of **Dixie Maru Beach** to the south.

Lanai

Generally considered Hawaii's most exclusive destination, Lanai is home to two large luxury resorts, one small hotel, and a handful of restaurants and shops, most of which are located in or around **Lana`i City**, the island's only town. The inland resort, **The Lodge at Ko`ele**, occupies the former site of Lanai Ranch and evokes a European woodland hunting lodge. Down on the

southern coast, the **Manele Bay Hotel** offers a more traditional tropical resort experience with a setting at Hulopo`e Bay, Lanai's best swimming and snorkelling beach. The only other accommodation can be found at Lana`i City's **Hotel Lanai**. Built in 1923 by Jim Dole to entertain important guests, it also houses a fine Cajun restaurant.

There are various sites to explore on Lanai by 4WD, although the dirt roads can be dangerous depending on the weather, so always seek local advice before you set out. The eastern wall of the central Palawai Basin has a rich collection of ancient Hawaiian carvings known as the **Luahiwa Petroglyphs**, accessible from the **Munro Trail**, a rugged, 20-mile (32km) dirt road that offers spectacular views of five other islands from the pine-lined ridge of Lana`ihale, the island's highest mountain (3,380ft/1,030m). The southwestern corner of Lanai houses

HAWAIIAN FISH-PONDS

Hawaiians were masters of aquaculture, or fish-farming, and built many large, coastal fish-ponds, the remains of about 60 of which survive along the southeastern coast of Molokai. Using lava rocks, long walls were constructed from the shoreline, enclosing several hundred acres of water and shallow reefs. Wooden sluice-gates allowed baby fish into the enclosure, but prevented them from leaving once fully grown, making harvesting a simple matter of wading through with nets. The fish raised in these ponds, generally mullet and milkfish, were destined only for the chiefs' tables – it was *kapu* for commoners to eat them.

the preserved ruins of an ancient Hawaiian village at **Kaunolu**, where a daredevil chief from Maui once survived the suicidal dive 90ft (27m) off the cliff ledge from his eponymous **Kahekili's Leap**.

The dirt track leading northwest out of Lana`i City leads down to **Polihua Beach**, a broad, windswept beach that offers views over the channel to Molokai (but is far too dangerous for swimming). Stretching for 8 miles (13km) to the east is Kaiolohia Beach, better known as **Shipwreck Beach**. A large 1950s tanker sits on the reef about a mile east of Polihua. You can also take the northeastern road from Lana`i City down past **Federation Camp**, a weekend fishing camp used by local descendants of the original Filipino plantation workers, and hike west a bit to see the rusting hull of a World War II cargo ship, believed to have been deliberately beached there after the war.

Molokai and Lanai

The secluded island of Lanai

Drive: The east coast of Molokai

This drive follows the coastline on the Kamehameha V Highway (Route 450) from Kaunakakai to its end at the beautiful amphitheatre valley of Halawa.

The road is only 28 miles (45km) long but takes well over an hour to drive due to its narrow, winding sections. Allow a full day so you can have a picnic lunch, swim at Twenty-Mile Beach and even fit in a horseback ride or valley hike (book in advance).

1 One Ali`i Beach ('Three-mile Beach')

The original name of this beach was Oneali`i ('Royal Sands'), but the typographical mix-up stuck. The water is too silty for swimming but the beach is an excellent place to launch a kayak, and there are picnic tables under the palm trees.

2 Father Damien's churches

Father Damien (*see p118*) built four churches 'topside', of which two remain. Seven miles (11km) on from One Ali`i Beach is the tiny **St Joseph's Church**, built in 1876 and featuring a statue of the priest. About 4 miles (6.5km) further down is the larger **Our Lady of Seven Sorrows Church** (1874), set back from the road behind a large wooden cross on the left.

3 Royal fish-ponds

This coastline once had more than 60 royal fish-ponds (*see text box p114*). Many have silted over, been lost to mangroves or just crumbled away, but some have been restored and are visible on your right as you drive – just look for the long lava-rock walls curving out from the shore.

4 Puko`o

This tiny town between mile markers 15 and 16 has the only store in east Molokai, a combination food market, general store, video hire and lunch counter offering plate lunches, sandwiches and smoothies (*open: Mon–Fri 8am–6pm, Sat & Sun 8am–5pm; lunch counter closed Mon*).

5 Twenty-Mile Beach

Officially called Murphy's Beach, this lovely strip of golden sand located just past mile marker 20 is better known by its numerical appellation. One of the nicest and safest beaches on the east coast, its shallow reef offers good swimming and snorkelling.

6 Pu`u O Hoku Ranch

Past Twenty-Mile Beach, the speed limit drops to 5mph (8kph) as the road narrows and serpentines past pocket-sized bays before climbing inland through the grassy ranchlands of Pu`u O Hoku ('Hill of Stars'), located at mile marker 25. A working cattle ranch and organic farm, they also offer accommodation and guided horseback rides (with 24hr advance booking) to nearby forests and beaches (*see p172*).

7 Halawa Valley

About a mile past the ranch, a widened bend offers a lookout over the beautiful Halawa Valley (*see p112*) before continuing for two final miles down to the valley floor. To the left, the tiny, green **New Jerusalem Church** is always open for quiet contemplation; or head to the right, park your car at the road's end and walk to the right for a few minutes to find a deserted pebble beach at the valley's mouth (unsafe for swimming). With advance booking, the owner of the **Halawa Tropical Flower Farm** (*see p173*) can take you on a guided hike to spectacular Moa`ula Falls.

Drive: The east coast of Molokai

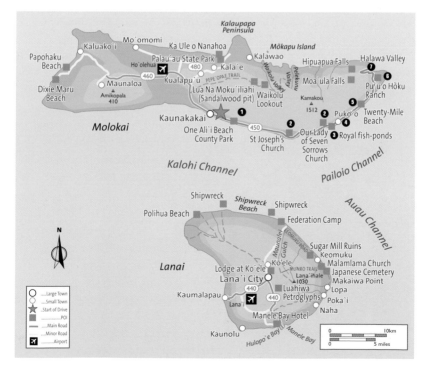

Kalaupapa and the Martyr of Molokai

The most devastating consequence of European contact was the many imported diseases brought over by foreigners, against which the Hawaiians had no immunity – about 95 per cent of the native population would die off in the century after Cook's first landing. No disease, however, was more feared than Hansen's disease (known then as leprosy). The first case was diagnosed on Kauai in 1835, apparently brought over from China by workers at the Koloa sugar plantation.

Within a few decades, it had spread to as many as 1 in 50 Hawaiians, and in 1865 King Kamehameha V decreed

Stained-glass monument to Father Damien

that all those suffering from the disease should be shipped off to Molokai's Kalaupapa Peninsula, one of the most naturally remote spots in the kingdom.

There was no real intention to care for these poor souls, but merely to isolate them from the population, give them a few meagre supplies and let them die off on their own. Taken from their families against their will, they were sent to Kalaupapa alone except for one volunteer *kokua* (helper) to care for them. The colony was then a wild and lawless place – ships, fearing to get too close, would drop people and supplies into the waters from offshore Mokapu Island, and those lucky enough to survive the swim would promptly be robbed of their things and forced to fend for themselves.

All this changed in 1873 when a young Catholic priest from Belgium, Father Damien de Veuster, came to visit the peninsula from his mission on the Big Island. He quickly requested reassignment. Over the next 16 years he cared for his charges personally, feeding and nursing them, dressing their wounds, and eventually burying

Father Damien's grave at Kalaupapa

them. He also used his considerable carpentry skills to build churches, houses, a school, a hospital and even a long irrigation pipeline to a valley stream to eliminate the arduous daily hikes for water.

In 1885, Father Damien himself contracted the disease, the only one of more than a thousand workers at Kalaupapa ever to do so. His mother expired of grief the day after the news reached Belgium, while the 'Martyr of Molokai' himself died in 1889 at the age of 49. His assistants Brother Joseph Dutton and Mother Marianne Cope continued his work at Kalaupapa, eventually moving the colony to a more permanent village on the other side of the peninsula, where safer boat landings could be

made. In the mid-20th century, new drugs were developed that could effectively cure Hansen's disease, and the isolation law was repealed in 1969.

Today the village is home to about 100 people: the few dozen former patients who have chosen to live out the remainder of their lives there, and various state and federal support workers. In 1936, Father Damien's remains were moved to Belgium – against his will – but his right hand was returned to Molokai in 1995, the year after he was officially beatified by Pope John Paul II. His name is still sacred to Catholics the world over and especially to the people of Molokai, who hope some day to see him become Hawaii's first saint.

Getting away from it all

Since the first stop for most visitors is Honolulu and Waikiki, some might think of Hawaii as a place full of bustling beaches and lively sidewalks. But anyone who ventures out of Waikiki will soon see that nature, not civilisation, is the essence of the Hawaiian experience. Although many of Hawaii's most beautiful and scenic spots might still see you surrounded by other travellers, there are plenty of more remote areas out there for you to explore.

OAHU
Kane`aki Heiau

This large 15th-century temple was built in honour of Lono, the god of agriculture. Archeologists have excavated and restored it thoroughly – complete with thatched huts and wooden statues – and although it's on private property, it's open for public visits on a limited schedule. Take Interstate H-1 west to Highway 93 and follow it up the leeward coast for about 20 miles (32km). Turn right onto Makaha Valley Road, bear left at the end, turn right onto Huipu Drive, and then right onto Maunaolu Street. Continue to the gatehouse and ask the guards for directions to the *heiau*; they'll ask to hold on to your driving licence or passport for security while you visit.

Mauna Olu Estates, Makaha. Tel: (808) 695-8174. Open: Tue–Sun 10am–2pm. Closed: Mon. Free admission.

Mauna Kea, Hawai`i the Big Island

Tantalus-Makiki Hiking Trails

Only minutes from downtown Honolulu are Oahu's finest trails, ranging from the suburb of Makiki Heights up the slopes of Mount Tantalus (2,013ft/614m). There are 18 interconnected trails; the first is a 2½-mile (4km) loop, which offers views of Honolulu and Waikiki through an abundant forest. Advanced hikers can venture further up to the Nu`uanu Pali Lookout (*see p49*) or Manoa Falls and the Lyon Arboretum (*see p43*). These are all at least moderately difficult hikes. Start at the **Hawaii Nature Center** (*tel: (808) 955-0100; www. hawaiinaturecenter.org*), located on a spur road off a hairpin bend in Makiki Heights Drive (½ mile/0.8km east of the Contemporary Museum). The centre offers trail maps and guided hikes on weekends, as does the **Sierra Club** (*tel: (808) 538-6616; www.hi.sierraclub.org*).

On the trail, Makiki Heights, Oahu

HAWAI`I THE BIG ISLAND
Green Sand Beach

Pu`u Mahana Beach, known as Green Sand Beach, is located 4 miles (6.5km) northeast of Ka Lae, the southernmost tip of the Big Island. The light green colour is due to the olivine crystals from a collapsed cinder cone above the beach slope. Most hire companies forbid driving their cars down South Point Road, although the road is actually safe. But only sturdy 4WD vehicles with high clearance can make the drive through the fields to get to the beach; otherwise it's an hour-long hike along the coast.

Mauna Kea

Standing 13,796ft (4,205m) tall, this extinct volcano is the highest mountain in the entire Pacific, making it one of the best astronomical centres in the world (and the only alpine region in the Hawaiian islands). Several companies offer guided afternoon trips to the summit in comfortable touring vans, with star-gazing sessions after dark down at the Ellison Onizuka Visitor Center (located 9,000ft/2,744m up). **Hawaii Forest** *Tel: (808) 331-8505. www.hawaii-forest.com* **Jack's Tours** *Tel: (808) 969-9507. www.jackstours.com* **Mauna Kea Summit Adventures** *Tel: (808) 322-2366. www.maunakea.com*

A river of clouds pours into the Haleakala Crater, Maui

MAUI
Haleakala National Park

One of the most singular places you'll ever see is the summit of Haleakala ('House of the Sun'), the massive, dormant shield volcano that forms the entire eastern half of Maui. In under two hours, you can drive to 10,023ft (3,055m) above sea level – temperatures can drop by more than 20°F (11°C), so bring a jumper no matter how hot the weather seems – to an otherworldly place of cinder deserts and alpine shrubland. Only at Haleakala can you look out over a giant crater with a floor blanketed by clouds, and see the famed Haleakala silversword – a plant found nowhere else on earth. It grows for up to 50 years, finally flowering just before it dies. For a breathtaking sight, book a sunrise tour; a comfortable van will drive you to the summit in the early-morning dark so you can catch the dawn's first rays as they burst over the crater.

Haleakala Crater Road (Hwy 378). Tel: (808) 572-4400. www.nps.gov/hale. Open: 24 hours, Park Headquarters 8am–4pm, Visitor Center 6.30am–3.30pm. Admission charge.

KAUAI
Koke`e State Park

Koke`e State Park covers 4,345 acres (1,758 hectares) of the forested, mountainous land in the northwest corner of the island, including the dense and massive Alaka`i Swamp, a depression at the base of Mt Wai`ale`ale filled with boggy vegetation and navigable only by a boardwalk trail.

Almost two dozen hiking trails range throughout the park, at lengths of ½–3¾ miles (0.8–6km). Trail information (and a surprisingly wide range of books for sale) can be found at the informative **Koke`e Natural History Museum** (*tel: (808) 335-9975; www.kokee.org; open: 10am–4pm; donation requested*), located on Hwy 550 near park headquarters, and the **Koke`e Lodge**, a gift shop and inexpensive restaurant serving breakfast and lunch. If you want to rough it, book in advance to stay in the park's inexpensive cabins (*tel: (808) 335-6061*), but be warned that accommodations are extremely basic.

Na Pali Coast State Park

Besides boat or helicopter, the only way to see the Na Pali Coast is by foot. The arduous Kalalau Trail (*www.kalalautrail.com*) runs for 11 miles (18km) from Ke`e Beach along the coast to the spectacular Kalalau Valley, the former hideout of Ko`olau the Leper, a fugitive memorialised in Jack London's eponymous story. A day-use hiking permit is required past Hanakapi`ai Valley, so most hikers just trek there and back, a 4-mile (6.5-km) round trip. (Do not attempt to swim here; many drownings have occurred in the beach's treacherous rip currents.) In clear weather you can also try the unmaintained trail into the valley that leads to Hanakapi`ai Falls, which adds another 4 miles (6.5km) to the trip. Give yourself a full day, wear sturdy shoes and bring food and water; there are no supplies to be had at Ke`e Beach.

The Na Pali cliffs from Koke`e State Park, Kauai

MOLOKAI
Halawa Valley

If you'd like to get away from it all and stay there for a few nights, the Halawa Tropical Flower Farm (*see p173*) offers accommodation in a clean, comfortable yurt (a large, circular tent raised off the ground) with modern furnishings, and includes use of a separate bathroom with outdoor shower and a kitchenette.

Halawa Valley, Molokai

Kamakou and Mo`omomi Nature Preserves

The top of the Kamakou ridge that takes up much of northeastern Molokai is covered by over 2,700 acres (1,092 hectares) of the verdant, untouched **Kamakou Rainforest Preserve**, which makes for an unforgettable hike. It contains more than 250 species of plants, of which 219 are endemic only to Molokai, as well as an infinite variety of native insects and numerous birds. The roughly 3-mile (5km) hike is along a narrow boardwalk that covers the **Pepe`opae Trail**, and at its end is a lookout with incredible views of the Pelekunu Valley, one of the spectacular but inaccessible 'amphitheatre' valleys that line Molokai's northern coast. The dirt road to the trail also passes by a fantastic lookout over **Waikolu Valley**, as well as the **Sandalwood Pit**, a deep hole dug to the exact dimension of a ship's hull, which Hawaiian labourers would use to measure their harvests in the days of Hawaii's former sandalwood trade.

If you prefer the beach to the forest, the **Mo`omomi Beach Preserve** covers 921 acres (372 hectares) of sand dunes and coastal lands on the northwest of the island, home to two dozen native plant species, as well as green sea turtles, owls and native shorebirds like the great frigate bird.

The **Nature Conservancy of Hawaii** offers monthly guided hikes (Apr–Dec) through both preserves through their Molokai Field Office. There is a hike fee charged for transport costs. Consult the website or email or call for more information (*tel: (808) 553-5236; email: hike_molokai@tnc.org; www.nature.org*).

LANAI

Lanai is secluded enough of a destination that you probably can't get much more 'away' anywhere else. Besides the options listed in the 'Molokai and Lanai' section (*see pp114–15*), you could opt to hike the full 8-mile (13km) length of Shipwreck Beach and back, but be sure to stick to the shoreline; the inland gullies are filled with thorny scrub. It's also possible (assuming you have a sturdy 4WD vehicle) to drive the 12-mile (19km) **Keomuku Road** along the eastern coast of the island; just head down to Federation Camp and follow the road to the right. You'll pass by **Maunalei Gulch**, Lanai's wettest valley, as well as the ruins of a sugar mill and a church that once belonged to a failed plantation at **Keomuku**, a Buddhist Japanese cemetery where the plantation's workers were buried after they were felled by disease, and the remains of the former settlements that once dotted this coast. By the time you pass through **Lopa** and through to where the road ends at **Naha**, you'll be able to see across to uninhabited Kahoolawe, the smallest of the Hawaiian islands, just off the southern end of Maui.

When to go

Here's the good news: there's really no bad time to visit Hawaii. Even though it has two distinct seasons of summer and winter, its tropical latitude and persistent northeasterly trade winds ensure year-round temperatures of around 72–80°F (22–27°C), moderate humidity, and an abundance of blue skies. Generally speaking, May to October (summer) is somewhat hotter and drier, while November to April (winter) is a little cooler and wetter. But no matter what time of year it is, there's a warm, sunny beach waiting for you somewhere in the islands.

The reason is the amazing variety of microclimates, or small, localised weather patterns, to be found on each island due to their unique mountain topography. The northeastern, or 'windward' (*ko`olau* in Hawaiian), sides get rain and cooler temperatures directly from the trade winds, while the southwestern, or 'leeward' (*kona*), parts beyond the mountains are hotter and

The Big Island's rainy windward side gets its fair share of rainbows

drier. One extreme, but not atypical, example is on the Big Island's windward coast, where Hilo – the wettest city in the US – gets 180in (4,572mm) of rain per year; and yet only 60 miles (97km) away on the leeward coast, hot and dry Puako gets less than 6in (152mm). The temperature, on the other hand, depends on elevation; the higher up from sea level you go, the cooler it will get, so that in the 37-mile (60-km) drive up to the summit of Maui's Mount Haleakala – about 10,000ft (3000m) above sea level – the temperature can easily drop by 30°F (17°C).

All this makes planning a vacation to Hawaii quite simple regardless of seasons. If you're seeking sunshine and sand, stick to the leeward coasts. If you're pining for rainforests and lush, green valleys, head windward. Or you can have both. All the islands are small enough that finding the weather you want is as easy as getting in a car.

The main other difference between summer and winter is their seasonal effect on the ocean. Summers usually see calmer seas and safer swimming, while winter winds can whip up the surf to amazing heights, especially up north, which is why Oahu's North Shore and Maui's Ho'okipa Beach are considered to have some of the finest surfing and windsurfing in the world, respectively. The ocean temperature stays warm year-round, but even in summer, swimming in Hawaii can be dangerous, so always follow ocean safety precautions no matter where or when you're visiting (*see p158*).

Like most other warm-weather destinations, Hawaii sees a definite surge in tourism from mid-December through March, often with a slight rise in airfares and hotel prices. June through July are also busy since the majority of visitors come from the mainland US and many people travel in summer during school holidays. 'Slow' months like April, May and September through November may see lower airfares but still bring in around 5 million visitors each (where in peak months it's a little over 6 million). In short, neither tourist seasons nor the weather tend to run to extremes.

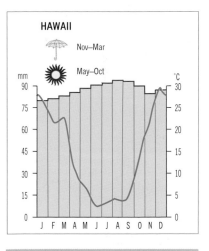

WEATHER CONVERSION CHART

25.4mm = 1 inch

°F = 1.8 × °C + 32

Getting around

Transportation is one of a traveller's main concerns when visiting Hawaii, and most visitors hire cars. Although the islands are not large, sights are spread out and you'll find your touring options very limited without a vehicle and may have to rely on hotel guest shuttles. And unless you plan on not leaving Oahu (where nearly all visitors arrive), you will need to travel to other islands, which is done almost entirely by short flight.

Around islands

Oahu, the most populated island, has an excellent public transport system that's sufficient for travel around Waikiki and Honolulu. It covers the rest of the island, but if you want to explore, you'll find a hire car faster and more flexible.

The other islands have no reliable transport system beyond a few hotel or local shuttles, so unless you plan to stay in one small town or resort, you'll almost certainly want to hire a car.

Bus

The routes of Oahu's excellent **TheBus** system (*tel: (808) 848-5555; www.thebus.org*) cover the entire island and especially areas of significant interest to tourists. See the website for

Oahu's bus system covers the whole island

It's slow going on some of Hawaii's winding coastal roads

maps and timetables, or ask your hotel for a system map. In Waikiki, routes run along Kuhio Avenue. TheBus also has two lines to and from the airport, but since large luggage items are not allowed on board (all bags must fit under a seat or on your lap), most visitors will need to use a taxi or hire car.

Fares are paid in cash (have the exact amount ready in notes or silver coins, as drivers cannot give change) or by pre-paid pass; at the time of writing, fares were $2 for adults, $1 for children 6–17 years, and free for children under 6 (when accompanied by a paying adult). Ask for a free transfer when you board; it's good for another ride within two hours. A four-day pass is available for $20 from any ABC Store in Waikiki, but isn't really worthwhile unless you

plan to take more than three rides per day. All buses are accessible to those with disabilities. All stops are indicated with a yellow 'TheBus' sign.

Car
Hired cars, vans and jeeps are the most popular way to get around the islands. Major companies include Alamo, Avis, Budget, Dollar, Hertz and National. Molokai has Budget and Dollar, while Lanai has only **Lana`i City Service** (*tel: (808) 565-7227*).

Drivers must be over 21 (or sometimes 25) and have a valid driving licence and a credit card. It's a good idea to book in advance. Rates begin at around $35 per day and some companies offer weekly discounts. There are also various daily taxes and fees, and unless your credit card or trip insurance covers it, you may want to opt for the Loss Damage Waiver (LDW), as under Hawaii law you will be responsible for any damage regardless of fault. Gas (petrol) stations can be far apart in remoter areas, so always fill up the tank when you get the chance and monitor levels carefully.

Roads in Hawaii are generally up to Western standards; certainly all highways and main streets will be fine, although some minor roads in rural areas may be unpaved or in inferior condition. Enquire with your car hire company about their restrictions regarding driving on unpaved roads. The speed limit on interstate highways is 55mph (90km/h), but otherwise is generally 25–35mph (40–55km/h); many narrow, winding coastal roads (such as Maui's Hana Highway or

Molokai's east coast) can go down to 5–10mph (8–16km/h).

Seat belts are mandatory for all riders, and pedestrians always have right of way. Right turns at red lights are permitted after a full halt, unless sign-posted to the contrary. Traffic in Hawaii, as in all US states, drives on the right.

Cycles

Bikes are available for hire in all tourist areas, generally for use around town (not long-distance touring). Another option is 'downhill cycling', where you and your bike are driven somewhere high up so you can ride back down without pedalling (Maui's Haleakala Crater is a popular option). Motorcycles and scooters can also be hired; helmets are required for riders under 18.

Taxi

Taxis can be hailed on the street in Honolulu and Waikiki; everywhere else they must be called. Although fares are metered, be sure to ask about approximate prices up front. From Waikiki to Honolulu International Airport, expect to pay $30–40. Tips of 10–15 per cent are customary.

Airport shuttles

The **Airport Waikiki Express** (*tel: (866) 898-2519; www.robertshawaii.com*) runs passengers from Oahu's airport to any hotel in Waikiki, leaving every 20–25

HAWAI'I VISITORS & CONVENTION BUREAU

This sign indicates a natural or historic sight of interest to visitors

minutes for $9 or $15 return. On Maui and the Big Island, the **SpeediShuttle** (*tel: (877) 242-5777; www.speedishuttle.com*) serves Kahului and Kailua-Kona airports respectively; call or see website for fares and reservations.

Between islands
Aeroplane
With the islands so close together, aeroplanes are the main method for inter-island transport for visitors and locals alike. Most flights are only 30–45 minutes long, although some routes require connecting flights through Honolulu. Five carriers and dozens of flights daily make for competitive pricing, so check websites for the best deals. Aloha and Hawaiian have the most flights and largest planes, and service all the islands as well as some US mainland and international destinations. Island, Pacific Wings/PW Express and go! feature mid-size and smaller planes and may be a better bet

for flights to Molokai or Lanai.
Aloha *Tel: (808) 484-1111.*
www.alohaairlines.com
go! *Tel: (888) IFLYGO-2.*
www.iflygo.com
Hawaiian *Tel: (800) 882-8811.*
www.hawaiianair.com
Island *Tel: (808) 484-2222.*
www.islandair.com
Pacific Wings *Tel: (888) 575-4546.*
www.pacificwings.com

Ferry
The giant SuperFerry sails passengers and cars from Oahu to Maui and Kauai (3 hours), with a route to the Big Island (4½ hours) scheduled for 2009. Two smaller ships also sail from Lahaina on Maui to Molokai (90 minutes) or Lanai (45 minutes).
Lanai Ferry *Tel: (800) 695-2624.*
www.go-lanai.com
Molokai Ferry *Tel: (866) 307-6524.*
www.molokaiferry.com
SuperFerry *Tel: (877) HI-FERRY.*
www.hawaiisuperferry.com

Mule rides are one form of transport to Molokai's Kalaupapa Peninsula

Getting around

Accommodation

As one of the world's top vacation choices, Hawaii is chock full of accommodation choices of every style, from campsites and hostels to B&Bs and top resorts. There are over 70,000 rooms across the six islands, with occupancy rates averaging around 80 per cent, so finding rooms to suit your vacation style, personal taste and budget should never be too difficult, especially since online booking is the norm for properties here.

Overall room quality conforms to Western expectations, and with few exceptions you'll find air-conditioning, ensuite bathrooms, TVs and telephones as standard, with many places also including an outside terrace (*lanai*) and small refrigerator or microwave oven as well. The average price of a hotel room across the state is around $200 per night, but that figure is inflated by Hawaii's high-cost luxury resorts; in reality, you can find reasonable rooms for closer to $100 per night, especially if you forego an ocean view or choose something further back from the beach. The most expensive rooms are found on Lanai, followed by Maui, Kauai, the Big Island, Oahu, and then Molokai.

Hotel rooms make up the majority of accommodation here, and all of the major international chains are well represented, many of which have huge resorts designed so you need never step outside the property. But most regular hotels have a pool and/or beach access, and are located in or near tourist areas, so there are plenty of things to do and see nearby.

If you're travelling in a group, your best value could be a condominium, or 'condo', an individually owned, furnished apartment with full kitchen, two or more bedrooms and a living room. Some properties may be located in regular hotels, with a pool, restaurant, 24-hour front desk and room-cleaning services, while others may simply be a flat in a standard apartment block (often with maid service). There are multitudes of websites that let you book online; try *www.royalhawaii.com*, *www.sunquest-hawaii.com* or *www.drhmaui.com* to start.

Those looking for something off the beaten path should try one of Hawaii's smaller inns or B&Bs (bed & breakfast), which may not always have the most modern amenities (ceiling fans instead of A/C, or no phone or TV), but are sometimes located in historic buildings or large homes, with individualised furnishings and the personal touch of an on-site owner. Many of these handle bookings through third-party websites such as *www.bestbnb.com* or *www.all-islands.com*

Nature lovers can camp in Hawaii's county and state parks, which require permits that are quite cheap or even free. Some parks also have inexpensive, basic cabins for rent, often booked out months in advance. For more information, contact the **State Department of Land and Natural**

Resources (*tel: (808) 587-0300; www.hawaii.gov/dlnr*).

Finally, budget travellers can find private double rooms in hostels for about $50 per night, although some have shared bathrooms. At the time of writing, Oahu and the Big Island have six or seven each, while Maui has two and Kauai has only one.

If you plan to hire a car, be sure to ask in advance about your accommodation's parking availability and fees.

The elegant lobby of the Princeville Resort on Kauai

Food and drink

Food in Hawaii has a poly-cultural panoply of flavours befitting its multi-ethnic society, featuring native Hawaiian, Chinese, Japanese, Portuguese, Mexican, Korean and American fare, and it comes as no surprise to learn that the fusion cuisine known as Pacific Rim was developed here. Fresh fish and seafood abound, as do locally grown beef, tropical fruits, and native vegetables and nuts, while caffeine lovers will get a volcanic jolt from Hawaii's world-famous Kona coffee.

Hawaii has plenty of restaurants to suit all palates and price ranges, although of course an area like Waikiki will have more options than a small town in a less touristy area. Restaurants often close earlier than you may be used to – except for Honolulu and Waikiki and some larger fast-food places, most stop serving dinner by 9pm.

To eat like a local, try a cheap, filling 'plate lunch', a meat or fish dish served with scoops of rice and cold macaroni salad. Other local dishes to look for include:

- *loco moco* – a breakfast dish consisting of a hamburger patty with a fried egg on top, served with rice and gravy
- *malasada* – a Portuguese doughnut, rolled in sugar
- *manapua* – a type of Chinese *dim-sum* (dumpling), with cured pork
- *poke* ('PO-kay') – a *pupu* (appetizer or snack) made of diced raw fish (often ahi tuna) with soy sauce, green onions and fresh herbs

- *saimin* ('SY-min') – soup with noodles and meat or fish

Finally, don't forget to try a shave ice, a huge dish of finely shredded ice flavoured with your choice of fruit syrups. It's unbeatable on a hot day.

Traditional foods

Here are some of the traditional dishes you may see on some menus, especially if you attend a *lu`au* (*see p137*).

- *kalua* – a pig wrapped in banana or *ti*-plant leaves and cooked all day with hot coals in an *imu* (underground oven)
- *laulau* – bits of fish or meat with taro leaves, wrapped and steamed in the *imu*
- *lomi-lomi* – sliced raw salmon marinated with tomatoes and onions
- *poi* – a purple-grey paste made from pounded taro roots
- *haupia* – a firm-custard coconut dessert

Vegetarians

Hawaii isn't really a vegetarian paradise. Fine dining tends to favour carnivores, although there'll often be at least one meatless option. Restaurants in the larger tourist areas will usually have garden burgers, pasta and salads on the menu. Shopping-centre food courts always have some kind of pizza or Asian-food options, but don't count on finding meat-free plate lunches. Natural-food supermarkets are common even in smaller towns and offer vegetarian foods and sometimes fresh salad bars or small cafés.

Drinks

Coffee lovers should not leave Hawaii without trying the local coffee, especially the 'Kona' beans. Restaurants and bars feature American and international wines and beers, but if you're interested in a local twist, Maui and the Big Island each have a winery and there are a number of small breweries, especially on Oahu, Kauai and the Big Island. Legal drinking age is 21.

Tipping

The standard minimum is 15 per cent in restaurants (unless service is included in the bill).

The Big Island is the home of world-famous Kona coffee

Food and drink

Entertainment

Music and dance are integral to Hawaiian culture, and you'll see live performances everywhere, from street buskers with ukeleles to local theatre groups to gala Polynesian dance revues. Much of Hawaii is still quite rural, so you'll find the greatest wealth of late-night entertainment options in Honolulu and Waikiki, followed by larger towns and big resort hotels on the other islands. For weekly listings, consult the Friday entertainment section of the Honolulu Advertiser *or local papers on each island, or grab one of the tourist magazines found at every airport.*

Bars and nightclubs

Night owls will find the greatest selection in Honolulu, especially Waikiki, which has plenty of bars and dance clubs that stay open well into the wee hours. Maui has some nightlife in Lahaina and, to a lesser extent, on the south coast, but don't expect the same range of establishments or the late hours of Waikiki; 10pm is popularly known as 'Maui Midnight'. Beyond Honolulu and Maui, don't expect much in the way of nightlife on the other islands. Some restaurants will stay open after the kitchen closes to serve drinks and offer live music, otherwise the most likely options will be bars and lounges in the larger hotels and vacation resorts, which often feature nightly live music to keep their guests entertained.

Cinema

Multi-screen cinemas (*see p146*) can be found on every island (except Lanai, which has a single screen). They're usually located in large shopping centres; check local papers or *www.moviefone.com* for listings. Besides the newest mainstream films from Hollywood and abroad, you can also find heavily discounted second-run movies (i.e. originally released several months prior) at **Restaurant Row** (*see 'Directory' listing, p141*) in Honolulu.

Many of Hawaii's preserved vintage theatres (*see 'Live performances' on pp138–9*) also show films. Depending on when you'll be visiting, you may also be able to attend some showings of the large **Hawai`i International Film Festival** (*www.hiff.org*), an island-wide event and the largest of its kind in the Pacific.

Cultural festivals

Bon Dances are held island-wide from late June through to the end of August to observe the O-Bon Festival, a

Japanese holiday in which Buddhists honour the spirits of their deceased ancestors. In Hawaii they've become a popular, midsummer-night's celebration of Hawaiian-Japanese heritage – an illuminated fairground filled with music, dancing, food stalls and costume displays open to all. A commonly held and touching ritual also sees the release of thousands of floating lanterns onto a body of water to symbolise the spirits of those who have passed on. Local advertisements will be posted, or check newspapers for listings.

Other fun events include island-wide Hawaiian cultural festivals, featuring *hula dancing*, *lei*-making, crafts, food and sporting competitions. The biggest of these are held on King Kamehameha Day (island-wide, 11 June), Aloha Week (island-wide, September–October) and the Merrie Monarch Festival in Hilo (April). The weekend closest to American Independence Day (4 July) also sees rodeo festivals celebrating *paniolo* culture on Maui (Makawao) and the Big Island (Waimea).

Lu`aus

Traditionally, a *lu`au* (feast) was held only on special occasions, such as a meeting of chiefs, but today huge *lu`aus* marketed at tourists are held several nights a week for up to hundreds of guests at a time. They're commonly found at larger restaurants, hotels and theme parks on the four main islands – if you don't see advertisements just ask at your hotel.

Besides an all-you-can-eat buffet of traditional Hawaiian foods (*see pp134–5*), they feature a full line-up of island-themed entertainment, including

A Polynesian dance performed at a *lu`au*

Beautiful flower garlands like these are made at Lei Day celebrations

a band of musicians, one or more singers and a troupe of dancers of both sexes performing *hula* and other Hawaiian and Polynesian dances. Some shows even end with a fire-dancing finale.

Many think of *luʻuas* as good-natured tourist fun, while others may find them unbearable kitsch. Either way, they're not cheap. They generally cost up to $75–90 per adult (which usually includes free-flowing tropical cocktails), and about half that for children, but you can usually find discounts through booking agencies and vouchers from tourist publications. The setting can often make all the difference – if possible, find one held outdoors by the beach instead of inside a dining hall or marquee.

Live performances
Oahu

Honolulu has the largest range of live performances in Hawaii, including theatre, opera, ballet, modern dance, and classical, rock and jazz music. The main arts venue is the **Neal Blaisdell Center** (*www.blaisdellcenter.com*), a modern, multi-venue centre where you can see touring Broadway shows, the **Honolulu Symphony Orchestra** (*www.honolulusymphony.com*) and the **Ballet Hawaiʻi** troupe (*www.ballethawaii.com*). It also runs the Waikiki Shell, an outdoor bandshell for music performances which has Diamond Head serving as a striking backdrop. Also in Honolulu is the **Hawaiʻi Opera Theatre** (*www. hawaiiopera.org*), the **Aloha Stadium** (*www.alohastadium.hawaii.gov*), which hosts large music concerts, and the classic, restored **Hawaii Theatre** (*www.hawaiitheatre.com*), which has a variety of music, dance and comedy performances on a regular schedule. Smaller theatre organisations include the **Diamond Head Theatre** (*www.diamondheadtheatre.com*) and the **Manoa Valley Theatre** (*www.manoavalleytheatre.com*), both of which run well-known musicals and plays, and the **Kumu Kahua Theatre** (*www.kumukahua.org*), a theatre for plays on Hawaiian life written by local playwrights. Tickets can be purchased in person, by phone or online directly from the venues, or else by phone or online through **TicketMaster** (*tel: (808) 521-2101; www.ticketmaster.com*).

Maui

In Maui, the main venue is the multi-million-dollar **Maui Arts & Cultural Center** (*www.mauiarts.org*), located in central Kahului. It has a comprehensive season of local and international musicians of many styles, classical music, modern and traditional dance, opera, theatre and other live performances. In nearby Wailuku, the vintage `Iao Theater (*www.mauionstage.com*) stages popular musicals and plays.

Hawai`i the Big Island

The Big Island has two vintage theatres that have been restored as venues for films and various live performances: the **Palace Theater** (*www.hilopalace.com*) in Hilo and the **Aloha Theatre** (*www.alohatheatre.com*) in Kainaliu on the Kona Coast. Up north in Waimea, the more modern **Kahilu Theatre** (*www.kahilutheatre.org*) offers a wide range of music and dance performances from both local and international artists.

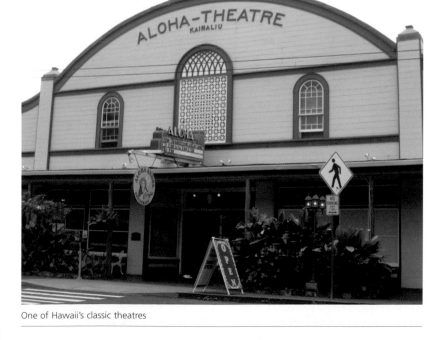

One of Hawaii's classic theatres

Shopping

Shoppers won't have to go far to find the goods; Hawaii abounds with craft fairs, main streets and shopping centres filled with souvenirs, jewellery, clothing, local produce and more. The main islands all have large, upscale shopping centres with major US and international brands, but even most smaller towns in Hawaii have open-air shopping plazas, and the main streets of tourist towns like Waikiki, Lahaina and Kailua-Kona are positively chock-a-block with shops.

Clothing

'Alohawear' – cotton and silk clothing with bright colours and bold patterns of flowers, *hula* dancers and Polynesian motifs – is sold everywhere, mostly as men's and women's shirts, but also as trousers and shorts, dresses and skirts, hats and the long, billowy *mu`umu`u* dress designed for Hawaiian women by scandalised Christian missionaries. The best-known store is **Hilo Hattie** (*www.hilohattie.com*), which features its own top-quality designs and has seven stores across the major islands.

Unsurprisingly, Hawaii is also a great place to shop for swimsuits and beachwear, and you'll find surf shops everywhere. It's also a dream for T-shirt lovers. The biggest T-shirt store is **Crazy Shirts** (*www.crazyshirts.com*), which sells them with everything from floral patterns to vintage logos and clever slogans, and specialises in shirts colourfully dyed from a range of unusual materials: coffee beans, wine, beer, chocolate, volcanic ash and even recycled US currency. Shirts dyed with local red dirt are also popular, especially on Kauai.

Convenience stores

With over 50 locations island-wide, the ubiquitous **ABC Store** is the tourist's best friend, especially in Waikiki (where the intersection of Kalakaua and Seaside alone has four stores). Most are open 6.30am–1am and sell deli foods, groceries, medicines and cosmetics, film, beach equipment, clothing and sandals, gifts, souvenirs, alcohol and almost anything else you could need.

Food and flora

Many of Hawaiian's agricultural exports are still popular gift items, such as local coffee (especially 'Kona' beans from the Big Island), pineapples, papayas, macadamia nuts, coconuts and tropical flowers and plants. Federal law strictly regulates the removal of fresh food and plants, so be sure to enquire whether your items can be taken home (pre-packaged 'take home' boxes that have already been cleared can be found at most airports). Some fruit, such as mangoes, guava or *liliko`i* (passionfruit), can never be exported fresh, but a variety of prepared foods like preserves, chutneys and dressings can be found and are perfectly fine to take with you.

Jewellery

Hawaiian *leis* made from *kukui* nuts, shells (the most valuable ones are from Ni`ihau) and silk flowers are popular, and you'll also find plenty of gold and silver in the upscale shops. Pearls are a local speciality, and many places (including Hilo Hattie) will harvest them in front of you from a bowl of fresh oysters; for a few dollars more, they can set them into a ring, earrings, pendant or brooch while you wait.

Shopping centres

Following is a list of some of the larger ones (often called 'malls') on the main islands:

Oahu

Ala Moana Shopping Center *1450 Ala Moana Blvd, Honolulu. Tel: (808) 955-9517. www.alamoanacenter.com*
Restaurant Row *500 Ala Moana Blvd, Honolulu. Tel: (808) 532-4750. www.restaurant-row.com*
Royal Hawaiian Shopping Center *2201 Kalakaua Ave, Waikiki. Tel: (808) 922-0588. www.shopwaikiki.com*

'Alohawear' features bright colours and floral patterns

Ward Centers *1240 Ala Moana Blvd, Honolulu. Tel: (808) 591-8411. www.victoriaward.com*

The Big Island
Prince Kuhio Plaza *111 East Puainako St, Hilo. Tel: (808) 959-3555. www.princekuhioplaza.com*

Maui
**Queen Ka`ahumanu Center** *275 West Ka`ahumanu Ave, Kahului. Tel: (808) 877-3369. www.queenkaahumanucenter.com*

Kauai
Kauai Village *4-831 Kuhio Highway, Kapa`a. Tel: (808) 822-4904.*

Sport and leisure

With lovely weather year-round and some of the most beautiful natural areas in the world, it's no surprise that Hawaii is a paradise for outdoor sports. The warm waters offer great surf and offshore reefs teeming with fish, so ocean activities are always a main draw, but there's plenty to do on land as well, whether you're looking for adventure, a leisurely pastime or the opportunity for a bit of pampering and relaxation.

There are far too many tour and equipment-hire companies around Hawaii to list in any guidebook, but beyond those in the 'Directory' listings (*see p160*), you'll see no shortage of brochures, leaflets and tourist-info magazines on display at airports, hotel lobbies and shops in tourist areas. Most markets are competitive, so it's not a bad idea to grab a few and call around to get the best price.

Boating

Kayaking is a popular and accessible activity here. Calm areas like Oahu's Kailua Bay or the Wailua River in Kauai are especially good, although there's also ocean kayaking, especially off the south coast of Maui. Outrigger canoe clubs have regular competitions; these are generally only for locals, except at Waikiki, where you can take a canoe ride with the local 'beach boys'. Many tour operators offer trips on catamarans and other yachts.

Cycling

Mountain bikes can be hired from sports shops in many tourist areas, although you'll need to ask about dedicated bike trails since cycles aren't allowed on hiking trails here. Popular spots include the North Shore of Oahu and the Polipoli Springs area of upcountry Maui. The newest activity is 'downhill biking', especially popular on Maui's Mt Haleakala, where a van drives bikers up to the summit so they can zoom the entire way down.

Fishing

Deep-sea fishing for yellowfin tuna, blue marlin and the like is popular here. The best area is off the Kona Coast of the Big Island, although you can also arrange fishing trips from Honolulu and Maui. Many locals cast directly into the surf for snapper and *ulua* (jackfish), but shoreline conditions can be dangerous to those unfamiliar with them, so always ask around at a local fishing store first.

Golf

There are almost 75 courses across all six islands of Hawaii, which hosts more professional tournaments than any other US state. Many are attached to luxury resorts. You can also find municipal, public or semi-private courses that charge less but often require advance booking. Kapalua on Maui has three beautiful courses, while Kauai's best can be found at Princeville and Po`ipu. If you fancy a challenge, try Oahu's Ko`olau Golf Club, rated as the 'toughest course in America' by the USGA.

Hiking

There are more hiking trails here than you can shake a walking stick at, and many organisations offer guided hikes. Some are discussed in 'Getting away from it all' (*see p120*); see the **Na Ala**

Hele Trail and Access System

(*www.hawaiitrails.org*) for more. Weather and trail conditions can be extremely variable and hiking to remote spots can be dangerous, so always research current conditions and local safety tips first.

Horse riding

Horseback tours are available on all the islands, either through individual operators, cattle ranches or even larger resort hotels. Molokai and the Big Island have some particularly good spots.

Scuba diving

The leeward sides of all the islands have coral reefs filled with fish and sea turtles, as well as submarine lava tubes, that all make for great diving spots. The best sites are found off Lanai, Maui and

Modern outrigger canoes are popular around the islands

Locals fishing from the surf on the Big Island's Puna Coast

the Big Island, although Kauai and Oahu have great locations, too.

Snorkelling

By far one of the most popular activities on Hawaii. Gear can be hired almost anywhere, or even bought cheaply at an ABC Store if you plan to go often. Top sites include Oahu's Shark Cove and Hanauma Bay, and Maui's Honolua Bay and Molokini Crater.

Spas

There are plenty of spas in Hawaii, both independent and attached to luxury resort hotels, offering a variety of massage styles, beauty treatments, therapeutic bodywork and yoga classes. A traditional form of Hawaiian

massage is known as *lomilomi*, in which pressure points are manipulated to release muscle tension and pain.

Surfing

Surfing was invented here centuries ago by Hawaiians who rode the waves on long wooden boards. The 7-mile (11km) stretch of surf on Oahu's North Shore is the world capital of surfing and home to the sport's top competitions in winter months.

But there are plenty of beaches with gentler waves for non-experts. One of the best is Waikiki, where you can get a lesson on the spot from the local 'beach boys' (and girls), just like in the old days. Surf shops offer individual and group lessons in other places such as the North Shore (in calmer summer seas) and the west coast of Maui, near Lahaina. Many good surfing and swimming beaches also offer great body-boarding (or boogie-boarding), where you ride waves close to shore while lying prone on a shorter board. These can be easily and inexpensively hired or bought.

Windsurfing (a surfboard with attached sail) is also popular in Hawaii. The mecca for experts is Maui's Ho`okipa Beach, but beginners can take lessons on the south and west coasts of Maui, in Hanalei on Kauai, and Kailua Bay on Oahu.

Swimming

Almost all hotels and resorts have pools, but of course Hawaii is known for its beaches. The ocean is warm year-round, and the safest swimming can generally be found along the islands' leeward shores or the windward coasts in summer. Waikiki Beach is a terrific swimming spot on Oahu, as are Lanikai and Kailua in the southeast. On Maui, head for the south coast and around Ka`anapali, and, on the Big Island, stick to the Kona and Kohala coastline.

Always remember that Hawaii's beaches can have dangerous currents and shorebreaks, and drownings do occur. See 'Emergencies' (*p158*) for ocean safety tips.

Tennis

The larger hotel and condo resorts almost always have tennis courts available for guests to use. Public and club courts are also available in most areas for court hire; check the directory listings or consult an activity operator.

Sport and leisure

Hiking trail in Koke`e State Park, Kauai

Children

Many people think of Hawaii as a romantic honeymooners' spot, but it's also a prime destination for families, with plenty of fun to be had for keiki *(children) of any age. Oahu has the largest number of child-oriented destinations such as aquariums, zoos and theme parks, but all the islands have incredible nature spots like waterfalls, volcanoes, and beautiful beaches, and most hotels, activity and tour operators will gladly cater to families of any size.*

When planning your vacation, look online for family packages, or enquire at your hotel or resort. You'll find plenty of coupons for discounts in the tourist magazines found at airports, in hotel lobbies and on the streets of tourist areas like Waikiki and Lahaina. With little ones, you need to take extra precautions against Hawaii's strong heat and seas. If it gets too hot, most large shopping centres and big towns have multi-screen movie theatres with air-conditioning and at least one child-friendly Hollywood movie available.

Larger hotels often have babysitting services for children. There are also private agencies that provide licensed, bonded and insured babysitters with CPR and first-aid training who will come to your hotel room. Ask your hotel concierge or consult an online search or telephone directory.

Cinemas
Oahu
Dole Cannery Stadium 18 Theater Complex *735B Iwilei Road, Honolulu. Tel: (808) 528-3653.*
Restaurant Row 9 Second-run movies show here for only $1 at night or 50¢ during the day. *500 Ala Moana Blvd, Honolulu. Tel: (808) 545-8635.*
Ward Stadium 16 *1044 Auahi St, Honolulu. Tel: (808) 593-3000.*
Windward Stadium 10 *46–056 Kamehameha Hwy, Kaneohe. Tel: (808) 234-4006.*

Hawai`i
Kress Cinemas Hilo *174 Kamehameha Ave, Hilo. Tel: (808) 961-0066.*
Makalapua Stadium Cinemas *74–5469 Kamakaeha Ave., Kailua-Kona. Tel: (808) 329-4461.*

Maui
Kukui Mall *1819 South Kihei Rd, Kihei. Tel: (808) 875-4910.*
WTC-Maui Mall Cinema 12 *70 East Ka`ahnumanu Ave, Kahului. Tel: (808) 249-2222.*

Kauai
Kukui Grove Cinema *4368 Kukui Grove, Lihue. Tel: (808) 245-5055.*
Wallace-Coconut Marketplace Cinemas *4–484 Kuhio Highway, Kapaa. Tel: (808) 821-2324.*

Molokai
Maunaloa Town Cinemas *1 Maunaloa Highway, Maunaloa. Tel: (808) 552-2616.*

Lanai
Lanai Playhouse Two shows per night Tue–Sun. *Seventh Street and Lanai Ave, Lana`i City. Tel: (808) 565-7500.*

Theme parks
Hawaiian Waters Adventure Park
This water-fun theme park has thrilling rides for adults and families, a wavepool, tubing river, children's area, cafés, shops, and even a mini-golf course, spread out over 25 acres (10 hectares) towards the leeward side of Oahu, only 30 minutes from Waikiki. Accessible by private transport, public bus, or combination private bus/admission packages. *400 Farrington Highway, Kapolei, Oahu. Tel: (808) 674-9283. www.hawaiianwaters.com. Open: Mon–Fri 10.30am–4pm, Sat & Sun 10.30am–5pm (hours subject to seasonal change). Admission charge. Bus: 40 or 40A from Ala Moana Shopping Center.*

Polynesian Cultural Center
Somewhat kitschy and inexpensive theme park with seven Polynesian themed 'villages' representing the traditional cultures of Hawaii, Samoa, Tonga, Fiji, Tahiti, the Marquesas Islands and the New Zealand Maori. Consult the website for the daily schedule of presentations of dancing,

The Wai`opae Tide Pools on the Big Island are a safe place for kids to snorkel craft-making and other entertainment, or come at night for the huge *lu`au*. *55–370 Kamehameha Hwy, La`ie, Oahu. Tel: (800) 367-7060. www.polynesia.com. Open: Mon–Sat 11am–9pm. Closed: Thanksgiving, 25 Dec. Admission charge. Bus: 55 (2-hour ride).*

Zoos and aquariums
Honolulu Zoo
Hundreds of birds, mammals and reptiles can be seen at this zoo at the eastern edge of Waikiki, in Kapi`olani Park, near the Waikiki Aquarium. Besides native Hawaiian animals like the *nene*, they also feature a large African Savannah exhibit and a children's petting zoo. On Sunday mornings, local artists display their works for sale along Monsarrat Avenue. *151 Kapahulu Ave (corner of Kalakaua Blvd), Waikiki, Oahu. Tel: (808) 971-7171. www.honoluluzoo.org. Open:*

Young or old, you can't beat a Hawaiian shave ice on a hot day

9.30am–4.30pm. Closed: 25 Dec. Admission charge. Bus: any eastbound from Waikiki.

Maui Ocean Center
This 3-acre (1.2-hectare) marine park features displays and exhibits on native Hawaiian sea life, including sea turtles, hammerhead sharks, lionfish, garden eels and Hawaiian wrasses. *192 Maalaea Rd, Wailuku, Maui. Tel: (808) 270-7000. www.mauioceancenter.com. Open: 9am–5pm, July & Aug 9am–6pm. Admission charge.*

Pana`ewa Rainforest Zoo
If you're driving to see the volcanoes, stop by this natural rainforest zoo for a free look at their little menagerie, which includes an alligator, iguanas, giant turtles, a pygmy hippo, peacocks, lemurs, and a giant white Bengal tiger with scheduled daily feeding at 3.30pm. *4 miles (6.5km) south of Hilo on Highway 11, Hawai`i the Big Island. Tel: (808) 959-9233. www.hilozoo.com. Open: 9am–4pm. Free admission.*

Sea Life Park
View daily performances by dolphins, sea lions and penguins, or even swim with the animals for an additional price. They also have a *lu`au*, the only one in Hawaii with a dolphin show. Located 15 miles (24km) from Waikiki at Makapu`u Point in southeast Oahu. *41-202 Kalaniana`ole Highway (Rte 72), Waimanalo, Oahu. Tel: (866) 365-7446.*

Building a transient masterpiece at Waikiki Beach

www.sealifeparkhawaii.com. Open: 9am–5pm (call for lu`au *schedule). Admission charge. Bus: 22, 58 (1-hour ride).*

Waikiki Aquarium

The third-oldest public aquarium in the US, known for its excellent exhibits on Hawaii's living coral reefs, with over 2,500 animals on display. Located at the eastern end of Waikiki in Kapi`olani Park, near the Honolulu Zoo, it's an easy walk from most area hotels, or accessible by public bus.
2777 Kalakaua Ave, Waikiki, Oahu. Tel: (808) 923-9741. www.waquarium.hawaii.org. Open: 9am–4.30pm. Closed: 25 Dec. Admission charge. Bus: 2.

Practical tips

- When booking accommodation, enquire about family suites or self-contained cottages. Many of the larger hotels and resorts also have special clubs and 'day camps' for children that are also available to non-guests.
- Take extra precautions to protect your children from the strong sun and heat. Use waterproof sunscreen with a high SPF, beach umbrellas, and brimmed hats and sunglasses, and always carry bottled water to drink.
- Hawaii law requires car seats for all children under 4 years old. Bring yours from home or request one when you hire a car. All vehicle occupants over the age of 4 are required to wear a seat belt.
- Ask about special children's menus and meal-time activity kits when eating out.
- Try *www.alohafriendshawaii.com/ keiki.html* and *www.travelsense.org/tips/children.asp* for more advice.

Sustainable travel

Responsible stewardship of the land and sea is a central ideal of traditional Hawaiian culture, and the demands of Hawaii's tourism industry can endanger the islands' resources. Below are some suggestions on travelling responsibly, or consult the websites Ethical Traveler (*www.ethicaltraveler.com*) and Partners in Responsible Tourism (*www.pirt.org*) for more ideas.

- Try to reduce your consumption and reuse or recycle where possible. Save electricity by turning off lights and air-conditioning when leaving your hotel room. Conserve water by asking staff not to replace your towels every day.

Buying fresh, local produce at a farmers' market helps support the local economy

- Respect sacred and cultural sites like *heiaus* (temples) by following the posted rules. Removing objects (such as rocks or offerings) from, destroying or otherwise altering a historic site in Hawaii is punishable by law and can incur fines of up to $25,000. Do not leave offerings of your own – this is considered offensive by native Hawaiians.

- Be aware of the environmental impact of your activities. Look into eco-friendly options like public transport, bicycles or walking. Reconsider visiting golf courses. Ask dive or snorkel operators if they use floats or moorings instead of anchors, which can destroy coral reefs.

- Never litter or leave objects behind when visiting beaches or natural sites. Unless properly disposed of, everything on an island eventually enters the ocean, where it can kill marine life. Keep some spare plastic bags handy for rubbish and cigarette butts, and help out by collecting any litter you come across.

- Coral reefs are living creatures and very fragile. If you snorkel or dive,

Proper disposal of rubbish is paramount on an island

take great care not to stand or step on coral, which can also cut and sting you. Look for sandy spots, or hire a flotation device along with your gear. Never remove any pieces of coral; it's protected by Hawaiian law.

- Never touch or feed any wildlife in Hawaii, either on land or sea, as this can disrupt animals' natural feeding patterns and make them vulnerable to accidents with automobiles or boats. Many animals also have defence mechanisms that could result in injury to yourself. Endangered animals, such as sea turtles and monk seals, are protected by Hawaiian law and it's illegal to touch or harass them in any way. Violators are heavily fined.
- State law prohibits taking plants and produce out of Hawaii, with exceptions for approved commercial products. If you'd like to take any flowers, fruits or plants home, look for those advertised as safe for export, which can be found in stores and airports.
- Support locally owned restaurants, shops and hotels when possible. Farmers' markets and craft fairs, held frequently in many areas, are a great place to find fresh food and beautiful souvenirs.
- Treat local residents with respect. Remember that your vacation paradise is their permanent home. 'Island Time' is more relaxed than what you may be used to, so don't get upset about slow service. Ask politely before taking photos of local people or their homes, and try having a friendly chat with some – you may learn something new that you won't find in any guidebook (even this one).

Essentials

Arriving and departing

By air

Nearly all visitors arriving by air land at Honolulu International Airport (HNL), located on Oahu, 10 miles (16km) west of Waikiki. The other islands' airports handle mostly inter-island flights, with a few US mainland flights going to the larger airports on Maui, Kauai and Hawai`i.

Maui has its main airport at Kahului (OGG), as well as small airstrips at Hana (HNM) in the east and Kapalua (JHM), near Lahaina, in the west. Kauai's main airport is in Lihu`e (LIH) on the east coast, with inter-island flights through Princeville (HPV) in the north. Most visitors to Hawai`i the Big Island fly into Kailua-Kona (KOA), although the windward side has Hilo International Airport (ITO). Molokai's small airport is named Hoolehua (MKK), and a tiny airstrip serves those taking a tour to Kalaupapa (LUP). Lanai has an airport in Lana`i City (LNY).

There are no departure fees from Hawai`i.

By sea

A number of major cruise lines offer trips to various islands in Hawaii, including Norwegian Cruise Lines (*www.ncl.com*), Princess Cruises (*www.princess.com*), Royal Caribbean International (*www.royalcaribbean.com*), Holland America Line (*www.hollandamerica.com*) and Cunard (*www.cunardline.com*).

Car hire

A number of US companies have offices at most of Hawaii's airports and large towns:

- **Alamo** *Tel: (800) 327-9633. www.goalamo.com*
- **Avis** *Tel: (800) 321-3712. www.avis.com*
- **Budget** *Tel: (800) 527-7000. www.budgetrentacar.com*
- **Dollar** *Tel: (800) 800-4000. www.dollar.com*
- **Hertz** *Tel: (800) 654-3011. www.hertz.com*
- **National** *Tel: (800) 227-7368. www.nationalcar.com*

Customs

Visitors over 21 years of age who are spending at least 72 hours in the US may bring in, duty-free: 1 litre of wine or spirits; 200 cigarettes, 100 non-Cuban cigars or 3lb of smoking tobacco; and $100 worth of gifts. Foodstuffs, produce and plants are not allowed. Sums of cash over $10,000 must be declared upon entry or departure.

Electricity

Hawaii uses 110–120V and the standard US plug with 2 flat parallel prongs. 220V appliances will need a step-down converter and a plug adapter.

Internet

Many hotels, restaurants and cafés offer free wi-fi internet to those with their own laptops. Larger hotels usually have internet terminals for guests – sometimes for an hourly charge. Internet cafés are neither common nor cheap. Some youth hostels offer their internet terminals to non-guests at lower prices. Public libraries have free internet terminals for patrons; visitors can obtain a 3-month library card for $10.

Money

Currency

The US dollar comes in notes of $1, $5, $10, $20, $50 and $100, all the same size and similar colour, so check your denominations before spending. One dollar equals 100 cents, with coins of 1 cent (known as a penny), 5 cents (nickel), 10 cents (dime) and 25 cents (quarter). Coin-operated washing machines take quarters, and telephones, vending machines and parking meters take all silver coins.

Cash machines (ATMs)

ATMs are plentiful and accessible 24 hours all over the islands, at banks, supermarkets, convenience stores and service stations, although many will charge a fee on top of your home bank charges. If you must use travellers' cheques, purchase them in US dollars and have your passport handy when cashing them.

Credit cards

All major credit cards are accepted just about everywhere on the islands, and most hotels and car hire companies will want an imprint of one for security. Most ATMs also accept credit cards for cash advances.

Money changers

Money-changing facilities are not widely found outside of Honolulu's airport and a few banks.

Opening hours

Banks Mon–Thur 8.30am–3.30pm, Fri 8.30am–6pm, sometimes Sat am.
Businesses Mon–Fri 9am–5pm.
Shops and restaurants Various, but generally around 10am–7pm, or 10am–9 or 10pm in Waikiki, tourist areas and large shopping centres (shorter hours on Sun). Some supermarkets and convenience stores are open around the clock.

Passports and visas

UK, Canada, Australia and New Zealand citizens need a valid passport, must stay less than 90 days, have a return or onward ticket and enter on an airline or cruise ship in the visa waiver programme (which includes all major carriers). US citizens need official ID to board a plane, such as a driver's licence. South Africans require a visa from their local US embassy (*pretoria.usembassy.gov*).

Pharmacies

Pharmacies are found in all cities and towns; **Long's Drugs** is the largest chain.

Post

All towns have a US Postal Service office or agent, usually open 8.30am–4pm weekdays and a few hours (variable) on Saturday mornings. Some hotels and gift shops also sell stamps. Postboxes are blue.

Public holidays

Hawaii celebrates all US national holidays as well as a few state holidays:
1 Jan New Year's Day
3rd Mon in Jan Dr Martin Luther King Jr Day
3rd Mon in Feb Presidents' Day
26 Mar Prince Kuhio Day
Mar/Apr variable Easter Sunday and Monday
1 May Lei Day
Last Mon in May Memorial Day
11 June Kamehameha Day
4 July Independence Day
3rd Fri in Aug Admission Day
1st Mon in Sept Labor Day
2nd Mon in Oct Columbus Day
11 Nov Veterans' Day
4th Thur in Nov Thanksgiving
25 Dec Christmas

Smoking

Smoking is prohibited in any enclosed public space or place of employment. Hotels usually reserve a few rooms for smokers, to be requested upon booking.

Suggested reading and media

Books

The Folding Cliffs by W S Merwin (fiction)
From a Native Daughter: Colonialism and Sovereignty in Hawaii by Haunani Kay Trask
Hawaii by James Michener (fiction)
Hawaii: A Natural History by Sherwin Carlquist
A Hawaiian Reader edited by A Grove Day and Carl Stroven (anthology)
Hawaii's Story by Hawaii's Queen by Lili`uokalani
Holy Man by Gavan Daws (Father Damien biography)
Letters from Hawaii by Mark Twain
No Footprints in the Sand: A Memoir of Kalaupapa by Henry Nalaielua with Sally-Jo Bowman
Paradise News by David Lodge (fiction)
Shoal of Time by Gavan Daws (history)
Travels in Hawaii by Robert Louis Stevenson

Newspapers and magazines

Hawaii has two state-wide newspapers, the *Honolulu Advertiser* and the *Honolulu Star-Bulletin*, and Hawai`i island, Maui and Kauai each have daily and weekly papers, while Molokai has two weekly papers. National and international papers can be found in major hotels and tourist areas.

TV and radio

Most hotel rooms have cable or satellite TV. Local and state radio stations generally feature classical and pop music, news and talk radio and Christian programming.

Websites

These are some helpful tourism sites:
www.gohawaii.com
www.visit-oahu.com
www.bigisland.org
www.visitmaui.com
www.kauaivisitorsbureau.com
www.molokai-hawaii.com
www.visitlanai.net

Taxes and tipping

Tax on goods and services is 4.17 per cent; for hotel rooms it's 11.42 per cent. Most prices are quoted *before* tax. Some hotels levy additional fees during high season.

Tipping is customary: 10–15 per cent for taxi drivers, $1 per drink in bars, $1 per piece of luggage for bellhops, $1 per night for housekeeping staff and $1–2 for valet parking attendants.

Telephones

Hawaii's area code is *808*, and the country code for the US is 1. To dial local (i.e. same island) calls, just dial the 7-digit number; to call inter-island dial *1-808* and then the number. For other US states, dial *1* then the area code and number. Toll-free numbers start with *800*, *888*, *866* or *877* and can be made free of charge from public phones.

Public telephones cost 50 cents for a local call. Pre-paid phone cards can be bought at newsagents and convenience stores. Directory assistance is *411* for local listings, or *1-808-555-1212* for listings on other islands.

To use an international mobile phone in Hawaii with a local SIM chip, you'll need a multi-band phone that will work on 850 and 1900MHz.

Time

Hawaiian Standard Time (HST) does not observe Daylight Savings Time in summer; the time difference thus increases by 1 hour for other countries using DST. For standard time, Hawaii is 2 hours behind the US west coast, 5 hours behind the US east coast, 10 hours behind the UK, 12 hours behind South Africa, 20 hours behind the Australian east coast and 22 hours behind New Zealand.

Toilets

Free public toilets are available in nearly all shopping centres, hotels and state parks. Some toilets are labelled in Hawaiian: *kane* (men) or *wahine* (women). Many beaches have portable toilets; BYO toilet paper.

Travellers with disabilities

Hotels, restaurants, buses and state parks have reserved parking, ramps and accessible toilets, and Avis and Hertz offer hire cars with hand controls if booked well in advance.
Disability and Communication Access Board *Tel: (808) 586-8121 V/TTY.*
www.hawaii.gov/health/dcab/travel
Society for Accessible Travel and Hospitality *www.sath.org*

Language

Overall, English is spoken as a first language here – Hawaiian is the primary language only on the island of Ni`ihau (*see pp108–9*). You will, however, see Hawaiian words on many signs and menus; *aloha* and *mahalo* are frequently used in everyday speech.

PRONUNCIATION

There are only 12 letters in the Hawaiian alphabet, namely six vowels, six consonants and two punctuation marks: a macron or horizontal bar (not used in this book) 'stresses' a vowel to indicate emphasis, and the `okina, or glottal stop, comes before or between vowels and is pronounced like the sound between the syllables in 'uh-oh'.

a – as in **a**bove (regular) / f**a**r (stressed)

e – as in b**e**t / ob**e**y

i – **y** as in pit**y** / s**ee**

o – as in h**o**le (but held longer)

u – f**u**ll / m**oo**n

h – **h**at

The consonants **k**, **l**, **m**, **n**, and **p** are pronounced as in English, the **w** as a **v** after an **i** or **e**, and as a **w** after **u** or **o** (the traditional pronunciation of *Hawai`i* uses the **v** sound).

COMMON WORDS

`aina	land
aloha	hello, goodbye, love
e komo mai	welcome, come in
hale	house
haole	foreigner, non-Hawaiian (especially white)
hula	traditional Hawaiian dance
kama`aina	resident, familiar ('same land')
kane	man
kapu	forbidden
keiki	child
kokua	help
kona	leeward
ko`olau	windward
lanai	balcony, porch
lei	garland (usually of flowers, feathers or shells)
lua	toilet, bathroom
mahalo	thank you
makai	toward the sea (*direction*)
mauka	toward the mountains (*direction*)
nene	Hawaiian goose (the state bird)
`ohana	family
`ono	delicious

paniolo	Hawaiian cowboy
pau	done, finished
wahine	woman
wikiwiki	quickly

OTHER WORDS

`a`a	rough lava
ali`i	noble, royal, chief(ess)
heiau	temple, place of worship
honua	land, earth
kahuna	priest(ess)
kapa	bark cloth
kapuna	ancestors, elders
koa	dark hardwood tree
kukui	candlenut tree
lomi lomi	traditional massage (*also* raw salmon dish)
luakini	temple of human sacrifice
maka`ainana	commoners
mana	spiritual power
mele	ancient song or chant
menehune	the oldest Hawaiians, according to legend a race of dwarfs
mo`o	lizard, dragon
mu`umu`u	long, billowy dress
nui	great, important
pahoehoe	smooth lava
pali	tall cliff
pua	flower

pu`uhonua	place of refuge
pu`u	hill
wai	water

MENU DECODER

`ahi	yellowfin tuna
aku	bonito or skipjack
a`u	swordfish or marlin
imu	pit oven for roasting pigs
lu`au	traditional feast
liliko`i	passionfruit
limu	seaweed
lomi lomi	raw salmon dish (*also* traditional massage)
mahimahi	whitefish or dolphin-fish (not a dolphin)
ono	wahoo
opah	moonfish
`opae	prawn
`opakapaka	blue snapper
`opihi	limpet
poi	paste made from taro root
poke	appetiser made of raw fish
pua`a	pig
pupu	snack, appetiser
saimin	noodle soup
uku	grey snapper
ulua	jackfish

Emergencies

Phone numbers

Emergencies (Police, Ambulance, Fire) *911*

Coast Guard Emergency *1-808-842-2600*

Embassies and consulates

All foreign embassies are in Washington, DC. Only Australia has a consulate in Hawaii.

Australia *(C) 1000 Bishop St, Penthouse Suite, Honolulu. Tel: (808) 524-5050. (E) 1601 Massachusetts Ave, NW, Washington, DC 20036. Tel: (202) 797-3000. www.austemb.org*

Canada *501 Pennsylvania Ave, NW, Washington, DC 20001. Tel: (202) 682-1740. www.canadianembassy.org*

New Zealand *37 Observatory Circle, NW, Washington, DC 20008. Tel: (202) 328-4800. www.nzemb.org*

South Africa *3051 Massachusetts Ave, NW, Washington, DC 20008. Tel: (202) 232-4400. www.saembassy.org*

United Kingdom *3100 Massachusetts Ave, NW, Washington, DC 20008. Tel: (202) 588-6640. www.britainusa.com*

Health risks

You don't need any vaccinations to visit the US, and Hawaii has little in the way of health hazards other than a few natural ones. **Mosquitoes** are a nuisance, but they don't carry malaria. Hikers should watch for **scorpions** and **spiders**.

Signs at beaches warn of dangerous ocean conditions

Ocean safety is extremely important. The waters are often very strong, especially in winter, and every year a few dozen visitors drown off Hawaii's shores. Always swim between the flags and in sight of lifeguards; if a beach is not guarded, assess water conditions carefully, stay close to shore and don't swim alone. Never turn your back on the ocean – sudden rogue waves can sweep you out to sea. Heed signs regarding dangerous rocks or coral, rips or currents and shore breaks. If you get carried out by a current, don't swim against it; wait until it dissipates, usually 100yds (90m) from the shore, then swim to either side, out of the current, and back to shore. If you cut yourself on coral, clean the wound thoroughly with antiseptic.

Sunburn and dehydration are always a danger in the tropics. Wear high-SPF sunscreen and protective clothing, and drink plenty of water. The sun is strongest 11am–2pm. Snorkellers should wear a T-shirt to protect back and shoulders.

Healthcare

Hawaii has Western-quality healthcare and facilities, and clinics or hospitals with emergency rooms can be found just about everywhere. Smaller islands have less extensive facilities; the best hospitals are in Honolulu. Your hotel can help you find a local doctor or dentist, or consult the local directory. Consultation fees usually start around $100, and even with insurance you'll need to pay up front and claim the costs back later. All hospitals and most doctors' offices will take credit cards, although smaller doctors' offices may prefer cash. Healthcare is expensive here, so travel and medical insurance is advised. Check for clauses on 'adventure sports'.

Crime

Violent crime is rare in Hawaii, but theft can be a problem. Never leave *any* valuables in a parked car, unless locked in the boot. Use common sense when walking alone at night. Use hotel safes to store passports, extra cash, jewellery and expensive electronics.

Police

In emergencies call *911*. For non-emergencies such as stolen property, go to the local police station.

If you are pulled over while driving, do *not* get out of the car; keep your hands visible until the officer gives further instructions. You will need to produce your driving licence and proof of car hire or vehicle insurance and registration. Do not attempted to bribe a police officer; it is a punishable offence.

Break-ins at car parks are common – never leave valuables in your car

Directory

Accommodation price guide

Prices are based on the lowest published rates for a standard double room per night, not including taxes and fees.

★	Under $100
★★	$100–$300
★★★	$300–$500
★★★★	Over $500

Eating out price guide

Prices are based on an average three-course meal, without drinks, for one person.

★	Under $25
★★	$25–$50
★★★	$50–$75
★★★★	Over $75

OAHU

Honolulu and Waikiki

ACCOMMODATION

Hale Aloha Hostel ★
The best budget option in Waikiki, offering clean, basic double rooms with private bathrooms in a quiet hostel only two blocks from the beach. Management is friendly and knowledgeable. Guests of all ages welcomed.
2417 Prince Edward St, Waikiki.
Tel: (808) 926-8313.
www.hiayh.org

Aqua Ocean Tower Hotel ★★
Steps from the beach, friendly service, comfortable, good-value rooms with free wireless internet and complimentary continental breakfast.
129 Paoakalani Ave, Waikiki.
Tel: (808) 687-7700.
www.aquaresorts.com

Royal Garden at Waikiki ★★
If you want to get away from beachside tourist crowds, this elegant boutique hotel near the Ala Wai canal offers a pool and sauna, courteous service and quiet, well-appointed rooms.
440 `Olohana St, Waikiki.
Tel: (808) 943-0202.
www.royalgardens.com

Waikiki Joy Hotel ★★
This centrally located boutique hotel, only a few blocks from the beach, doesn't have the most modern décor, but the service is friendly and all the rooms feature Jacuzzi tubs.
320 Lewers St, Waikiki.
Tel: (808) 923-2300.
www.aston-hotels.com

Sheraton Moana Surfrider ★★★
Waikiki's oldest hotel (built in 1901) still has the last word in understated elegance, with beautifully refurbished rooms and high-quality amenities and the area's best beachside location.
2365 Kalakaua Ave, Waikiki. Tel: (808) 922-3111. www.sheraton.com

Eating Out

Pho Old Saigon ★

This unassuming little place has brusque service but great Vietnamese food, with several varieties of *pho* (noodle soup).
2270 Kuhio Ave, Waikiki.
Tel: (808) 922-2668.
Open: 10am–10pm.

Brasserie du Vin ★★

Transport yourself to the south of France at this celebrated downtown café, featuring seafood specials, artisanal cheeses, French-style *tapas* and a wine cellar boasting over 250 different labels.
1115 Bethel St, Honolulu.
Tel: (808) 545-1115.
www.brasserieduvin.com.
Open: Mon–Wed 11am–11pm, Thur–Sat 11am–midnight, Sun 11am–4pm.

Keo's in Waikiki ★★

One of Honolulu's top Thai restaurants, with tasty noodle and seafood dishes and reasonable prices. Also serves American breakfast foods and has two other locations around Waikiki.
2028 Kuhio Ave,
Tel: (808) 951-9355.
www.keosthaicuisine.com.

Open: Sun–Thur 7am–2pm & 5–10.30pm, Fri–Sat 7am–2pm & 5–11pm.

Sansei Seafood Restaurant & Sushi Bar ★★

Award-winning Japanese and Pacific Rim cuisine features signature dishes like Japanese calamari salad and mango-crab hand rolls. Also has late-night dining specials and free karaoke on weekends.
Waikiki Beach Marriott, 2552 Kalakaua Ave, Waikiki. Tel: (808) 931-6286. www.sanseihawaii.com. Open: Sun–Thur 5.30–10pm, Fri–Sat 5.30pm–1am.

Soul de Cuba Cafe ★★

Cuban favourites like *ropa vieja* (shredded beef) and fricasseed chicken served in a cosy dining room filled with Afro-Cuban artworks and atmospheric salsa and jazz music.
1121 Bethel St, Honolulu.
Tel: (808) 545-2822.
www.souldecuba.com.
Open: Mon–Thur 11.30am–10pm, Fri–Sat 11.30am–11pm.
Closed: Sun.

Matteo's ★★★

Consistently voted one of Hawaii's best Italian restaurants, Matteo's offers classic fare like antipasto, seafood and veal dishes at market prices, with over 700 wines to choose from.
Marine Surf Hotel, 364 Seaside Ave, Waikiki.
Tel: (808) 922-5551.
www.matteoshawaii.com.
Open: 5.30–11pm.

Entertainment

Duke's Canoe Club

This popular family restaurant features a cocktail bar with live Hawaiian music every night from 4 to 6pm and 10pm to midnight, plus concerts on the beach on weekends.
Outrigger Waikiki Hotel, 2335 Kalakaua Ave, Waikiki.
Tel: (808) 923-0711.
www.dukeswaikiki.com.
Open: 11am–midnight.

Hank's Café

This small but boisterous bar and art gallery in Chinatown offers a friendly crowd and nightly live music, with local musicians playing everything from jazz to contemporary Hawaiian.

1038 Nu`uanu St,
Honolulu. Tel: (808) 526-
1410. Open: Mon 3–10pm,
Tue–Sun 3pm–2am.

Lotus Soundbar

Three-level club with five
swanky rooms featuring
international DJs
spinning house, lounge,
soulful hip-hop and funk.
2301 Kuhio St, Waikiki.
Tel: (808) 924-1688.
www.lotusoundbar.com.
Open: 9pm–4am.

SPORT AND LEISURE

**Jack's Circle Island
Adventure Tour**

Jack, a local expert in
Hawaiian history,
culture, wildlife, botany
and geology, takes only
ten guests for a small and
personalised full-day
tour covering the
southeast, windward and
north coasts of Oahu.
Book through the Hale
Aloha Hostel, Waikiki.
2417 Prince Edward St.
Tel: (808) 926-8313.
Tours: Mon, Wed, Fri
10am–9pm.

The north shore

ACCOMMODATION

**Ke Iki Beach
Bungalows ★★**

Comfortable bungalows
with one or two
bedrooms, full kitchen
and cable TV, some
located right on the
beach, where you can
watch the sun set from
your private deck.
59–579 Ke Iki Rd, Sunset
Beach. Tel: (808) 638-
8229. www.keikibeach.com

Turtle Bay Resort ★★★★

A full-service luxury
resort with three pools,
two golf courses, a spa,
horse stables, ten tennis
courts and three
restaurants. All rooms
feature a private lanai
and an ocean view.
57–091 Kamehameha
Hwy, Kahuku.
Tel: (808) 293-8811.
www.turtlebayresort.com

EATING OUT

Chocolate Gecko ★

For a caffeine and sugar
hit, try this café for fresh
espresso, Italian sodas
and chocolate truffles.
66–470 Kamehameha
Hwy, Hale`iwa. Tel: (808)
637-9104. Open:
Wed–Mon 11am–5pm.
Closed: Tue.

**Cholo's Homestyle
Mexican ★**

Fresh Mexican food in a
jauntily decorated
restaurant in the North
Shore Marketplace. Gets
popular at night, when
the full-service bar stays
open until 11pm.
66–250 Kamehameha
Hwy, Hale`iwa.
Tel: (808) 637-3059.
www.cholosmexican.com.
Open: 11am–9.30pm.

Spaghettini ★

A dozen varieties of New
York-style pizzas sold by
the pie or slice, pasta
dishes and other Italian
fare at this popular,
family-owned eatery.
66–200 Kamehameha
Hwy, Hale`iwa.
Tel: (808) 637-0104.
Open: 11am–8pm.

**Jameson's by the
Sea ★★★**

Oceanfront dining on
Jameson's large lanai is
unbeatable at sunset. The
menu offers mostly
American cuisine,
specialising in fish,
seafood and steaks plus
soups and salad.
62–540 Kamehameha
Hwy, Hale`iwa.
Tel: (808) 637-4336.
www.
jamesonshawaii.com.
Open: Mon–Fri 11am–
9.30pm, Sat–Sun
9am–9.30pm.

Sport and leisure
Surf 'n' Sea
The North Shore's biggest surf shop also offers a wide range of activities: surfing and body-boarding lessons, diving and snorkelling, and fishing and seasonal whale-watching trips.
62–595 Kamehameha Hwy, Hale`iwa. Tel: (808) 637-9887.
www.surfnsea.com

Southeast and windward Oahu
Accommodation
Lanikai Beach Rentals ★★
Offers several nicely appointed bungalows, studios to two bedrooms, with all mod cons, located only a few minutes' walk to Lanikai Beach. Also has properties near Kailua Beach.
1277 Mokulua Dr, Lanikai. Tel: (808) 261-7895. www. lanikaibeachrentals.com

Eating out
Assaggio Italian Restaurant ★★
A casual atmosphere and large portions of pastas, seafood and grilled meats make this one of the area's most popular Italian restaurants.
354 Uluniu St, Kailua. Tel: (808) 261-2772. Open: Tue–Thur 11.30am–2.30pm & 5–9.30pm, Fri–Sat 11.30am–2.30pm & 5–10pm, Sun 5–9.30pm.

Sport and leisure
Kualoa Ranch
This former cattle ranch offers horseback and ATV tours of its extensive grounds on the windward coast.
Hwy 83, Kualoa. Tel: (800) 237-7321. www.kualoa.com

HAWAI`I THE BIG ISLAND
The Kona Coast
Accommodation
Manago Hotel ★
A popular budget choice, this family hotel, running since 1917, offers basic but clean rooms with fantastic coastal views from its higher floors, as well as a friendly, inexpensive restaurant.
Hwy 11, Captain Cook. Tel: (808) 323-2642. www.managohotel.com
Castle Kona Reef ★★
Popular ocean-front condo-hotel within walking distance of Kailua's shops. Has self-contained one or two-bedroom suites with all the mod cons and swimming pool. Discounted rates for online booking.
75–5888 Ali`i Drive, Kailua-Kona. Tel: (808) 329-2959.
www.castleresorts.com
Ka`awaloa Plantation ★★
This huge, beautiful plantation house perched above Kealekekua Bay offers five tastefully decorated bedrooms (including a large suite), most with ocean views. Included breakfast features fresh fruit from the grounds and hot dishes.
82–5990 Napoopoo Rd, Captain Cook. Tel: (808) 323-2686. www. kaawaloaplantation.com
Royal Kona Resort ★★
Large, multi-building hotel located right on Kailua Bay. Great location and 450 rooms with modern amenities. The standard Bay Tower rooms are pretty ordinary – it's worth paying extra for one of the recently

refurbished ones in the Ali`i Tower instead.
75–5852 Ali`i Drive, Kailua-Kona.
Tel: (808) 329-3111.
www.hawaiianhotels.com

EATING OUT

Aloha Angel Café ★/★★
Large, friendly restaurant located in the classic Aloha Theatre building. A comprehensive menu offers breakfast, lunch and dinner (with good vegetarian options) made with local ingredients, and desserts baked daily on the premises.
Aloha Theatre, Hwy 11, Kainaliu.
Tel: (808) 322-3383.
www.alohatheatre.com.
Open: 7.30am–8.30pm.

Fujimama's ★★
Snazzy Japanese restaurant with friendly service, fresh seafood and killer cocktails. Also offers a good-value lunch special.
75–5719 Ali`i Dr, Kailua-Kona. Tel: (808) 327-2125.
www.fujimamas.com

Kona Inn Restaurant ★★
Located in the former Kona Inn (1928), this seafood and steak restaurant offers open-air dining on a large terrace

over the bay, right in the middle of town.
Kona Inn Shopping Village, 75–5744 Ali`i Dr.
Tel: (808) 329-4455.
Open: 11.30am–9.30pm.

SPORT AND LEISURE

Kings' Trail Rides
Half-day horseback rides down to Kealekekua Bay, including snorkelling time and picnic lunch.
Hwy 11, Kealekekua.
Tel: (808) 323-2388.
www.konacowboy.com

Ocean Eco Tours
Offers diving/snorkelling trips, surfing lessons and whale-watching tours (in season).
74–425 Kealakehe Pkwy, Kailua-Kona.
Tel: (808) 324-7873.
www.oceanecotours.com

Hilo and the southeast

ACCOMMODATION

Dolphin Bay Hotel ★★
A good bargain hotel for a Hilo base. The friendly management offers studios and one- and two-bed rooms with full kitchens, although there's no pool or restaurant. Located just outside of downtown, so you'll want a car.

333 Iliahi St, Hilo.
Tel: (808) 935-1466.
www.dolphinbayhotel.com

Hilo Hawaiian Hotel ★★
This once-grand dame of Banyan Drive may be slightly faded but still offers large, comfortable rooms with fantastic views of Hilo Bay, just down the road from Lili`uokalani Gardens. Downtown is a bit of a walk, so a car will be helpful here.
71 Banyan Dr, Hilo.
Tel: (808) 935-9361.
www.castleresorts. com/hhh/

The Inn at Volcano ★★
Deluxe themed rooms and suites located just outside Volcanoes National Park, with breakfast and wi-fi included. Standard and budget accommodations also offered nearby.
Wright Rd & Laukapu Rd, Volcano. Tel: (808) 967-7786. www.volcano-hawaii.com

Kalani Oceanside Retreat ★★
A new-age wellness retreat featuring daily yoga classes, dance workshops, and fresh fish and vegetarian buffet

meals, also with a large pool, Jacuzzis and a sauna. Located in a tranquil setting on the Puna Coast.
Hwy 137, Pahoa.
Tel: (808) 965-7828.
www.kalani.com

Shipman House B&B Inn ★★

This magnificent Victorian mansion (1899) is filled with antiques and once hosted both Jack London and Queen Lili`uokulani. Offers five bedrooms and breakfast with fresh fruit grown on the property.
131 Ka`iulani St, Hilo.
Tel: (808) 934-8002.
www.hilo-hawaii.com

EATING OUT

Blane's Drive Inn ★

A classic American fast-food joint, with cheap and filling fare like burgers, plate lunches, *loco moco* and *saimin*.
217 Waianuenue Ave, Hilo. Tel: (808) 969-9494.
Open: Mon–Sat 5am–9pm, Sun 6am–9pm.

Café Pesto ★★

A Big Island favourite, with two branches offering Italian favourites like gourmet pizzas,

calzones, risottos and pasta as well as a few Asian-inspired mains and homemade desserts.
308 Kamehameha Ave, Hilo. Tel: (808) 969-6640. Kawaihae Center, Kawaihae. Tel: (808) 882-1071. www.cafepesto.com. Open: Sun–Thur 11am–9pm, Fri–Sat 11am–10pm.

Restaurant Kaikodo ★★★

Hilo's finest restaurant, located in the restored 1908 Toyama Building, has Asian and Italian-influenced dishes like sesame-crusted *ahi* and seared loin of lamb in balsamic vinegar.
60 Keawe St. Tel: (808) 961-2558. www. restaurantkaikodo.com. Open: Tue–Thur 11am–2pm & 5.30–9pm, Fri 11am–2pm & 5.30–9.30pm, Sat 5.30–9pm. Closed: Sun, Mon.

ENTERTAINMENT

The Emerald Orchid ★★

This upscale Irish bar boasts a large food menu, ten beers on tap (including Guinness and five local brews), dozens of whiskeys and live music or DJs most nights,

including Hawaiian music once a week.
168 Keawe St, Hilo.
Tel: (808) 961-5400.
Open: 11am–2am.

Kohala and the north
ACCOMMODATION
Kohala Village Inn ★

This plantation-style hotel offers 19 rooms, with pleasant island décor and refurbished private bathrooms, along with satellite TV, free breakfast, wireless internet and an on-site restaurant.
55–514 Hawi Rd, Hawi.
Tel: (808) 889-0404. www. kohalavillageinn.com

'Aaah, the Views!' B&B ★★★

You'll believe the name when you look out of the windows of this well-appointed private B&B. The hosts offer top hospitality and delicious breakfasts.
66–1773 Alaneo St, Waimea.
Tel: (808) 885-3455.
www.aaahtheviews.com

Hapuna Beach Prince Hotel ★★★

One of the Kohala Coast's top resorts, with on-site spa and fitness centre, golf course designed by Arnold Palmer and beautiful beach and pool areas. Sign up to their free 'preferred guest' club online to get better rates. *62–100 Kauna`oa Drive, Kohala Coast. Tel: (808) 880-1111. www.hapuna beachprincehotel.com*

Eating out
Bamboo Restaurant and Bar ★★
Healthy portions of auntie-cooked 'island-style' cuisine, made with local ingredients, are served here in this Big Island favourite, located in a classic hotel on Hawi's main street. Live music offered regularly. *Hwy 270, Hawi. Tel: (808) 889-5555. www. bamboorestaurant.info. Open: Tue–Sat 11.30am– 2.30pm & 6–9pm, Sun 11am–2pm. Closed: Mon.*
Café Pesto ★★
Listed above (*see 'Hilo and the southeast' p165*).
Kawaihae Harbor Grill ★★
An upscale restaurant in a pleasantly vintage, green wooden building on Kawaihae Harbor

(unfortunately lacking a view). Mostly Italian-cuisine seafood and beef, with one vegetarian option. *Off Hwy 270, Kawaihae. Tel: (808) 882-1368. www.kawaihae-restaurants.com. Open: 7am–11am, 11.30am– 2.30pm & 5.30–9.30pm.*
Sushi Rock ★★
Small, modern café featuring signature sushi rolls made with local ingredients, and other updates on traditional Japanese fare. *Hawi Hale Building, Hawi. Tel: (808) 889- 5900. Open: Mon, Tue, Thur, Sun noon–3pm & 5.30–8pm, Fri–Sat noon–3pm & 5.30–9pm. Closed: Wed.*

MAUI
The west side
Accommodation
Lahaina Inn ★★
This boutique hotel, in a restored classic building, offers individually decorated rooms with charming Victorian décor, just above David Paul's Lahaina Grill. *127 Lahainaluna Rd, Lahaina.*

Tel: (808) 661-0577. www.lahainainn.com
The Plantation Inn ★★
Romantic plantation house offers 15 rooms and 4 suites with individual décor and all mod cons, and a quiet central courtyard with pool and Jacuzzi. A fine French restaurant is located on the ground floor. *174 Lahainaluna Rd, Lahaina. Tel: (808) 667- 9225. www. theplantationinn.com*
Outrigger Napili Shores ★★
Comfortable beachside condo resort with newly refurbished, fully equipped studio and one-bedroom apartments. *5315 Lower Honoapiilani Rd, Napili Bay. Tel: (808) 669-8061. www.outrigger.com*
Royal Lahaina Resort ★★
Top resort with the best location on Ka`anapali Beach, with 350 newly refurbished rooms and suites, two restaurants, three pools, eleven tennis courts and a nightly beachfront *lu`au. 2780 Keka`a Dr, Ka`anapali.*

Tel: (808) 661-3611.
www.2maui.com

EATING OUT
Lahaina Fish Co. ★★
Fresh Hawaiian fish and
steaks served open-air on
a dining *lanai* over the
harbour.
831 Front St, Lahaina.
Tel: (808) 661-3472.
Open: 11am–10pm.
David Paul's Lahaina Grill ★★★
Voted 'Maui's Best
Restaurant' every year
since 1994. Serves 'New
American' cuisine with a
wide range of meat, fish
and pasta dishes, with an
impressive wine list.
127 Lahainaluna Rd,
Lahaina.
Tel: (808) 667-5117.
www.lahainagrill.com.
Open: 6–9.15pm.

ENTERTAINMENT
Warren and Annabelle's Magic Show
Crowd-pleasing show
(with drinks and dinner
available) hosting a
rotating schedule of
performers.
900 Front St, Lahaina.
Tel: (808) 667-6244. www.
warrenandannabelles.com.
Open: Mon–Sat 5pm &

7.30pm. Reservations
required. Ages 21 and
older only.

SPORT AND LEISURE
Outrageous Surf
Daily surfing classes for
all levels, in small groups
or one-on-one.
640 Front St, Lahaina.
Tel: (808) 669-1400.
www.youcansurf.com
Pacific Whale Foundation
Maui's oldest marine
research and conservation
organisation offers a
variety of sea-based trips
including snorkelling,
leisure cruises and whale-
spotting tours.
612 Front St, Lahaina.
Tel: (808) 249-8811.
www.pacificwhale.org

The south coast
ACCOMMODATION
Mana Kai Maui ★★
Great-value hotel rooms
and self-contained one-
or two-bedroom condo
units located beside
the beach at Kihei's
southern end, with an
excellent restaurant
downstairs.
2960 S Kihei Rd, Kihei.
Tel: (808) 879-2778.
www.crhmaui.com

Maui Coast Hotel ★★
Comfortable, modern
hotel rooms and one-
bedroom suites located
across the road from
Kama`ole Beach #1, with
a large outdoor pool and
tennis courts.
2259 S Kihei Road, Kihei.
Tel: (808) 874-6284.
www.mauicoasthotel.com

SPORT AND LEISURE
Maui Thrills EcoNature Ocean Tours
Independent, eco-
conscious tour operator
offering many choices for
local snorkelling,
kayaking, sailing and
custom-designed trips.
Kihei. Tel: (808) 875-6181.
www.mauithrills.com

The north coast and upcountry
ACCOMMODATION
The Inn at Mama's Fish House ★★
These six comfortable
one- and two-bedroom
cottages are set between
a lovely beach and the
popular eponymous
restaurant. Polynesian-
themed décor, all
modern conveniences,
full kitchens and daily
maid service.

799 Poho Pl, Paia. Tel: (808) 579-9764. www. mamasfishhouse.com

Kula Lodge ★★

This rustic upcountry lodge offers five mountainside chalets with queen beds and private *lanais*; four have sleeping lofts with extra twin beds. Art gallery, crafts shops and a fine restaurant also on-site. *15200 Haleakala Hwy (Hwy 377), Kula. Tel: (808) 878-1535. www.kulalodge.com*

EATING OUT

Café Mambo ★

Friendly, modern-style diner with a full menu: omelettes and pancakes, burritos and fajitas, salads and burgers and even tagines and tapas. Great vegetarian options, too. *30 Baldwin Ave, Pa`ia. Tel: (808) 579-8021. Open: 8am–9pm.*

Kula Lodge ★★

Upscale but very reasonable upcountry restaurant with Hawaii-influenced continental fare like *Mahi-mahi* piccata and mango-braised ribs, along with a decent number of vegetarian options and some delicious desserts. *15200 Haleakala Hwy (Hwy 377), Kula. Tel: (808) 878-1535. www.kulalodge.com. Open: 6.30am–8.30pm.*

Makawao Steak House ★★

This atmospherically rustic restaurant, housed in a 1920s building, grills up large portions of local steak, ribs, poultry and seafood, accompanied by plenty of sides. *3612 Baldwin Ave, Makawao. Tel: (808) 572-8711. Open: Tue–Sun 5.30–9.30pm. Closed: Mon.*

ENTERTAINMENT

Casanova

Three nights a week, this Italian restaurant becomes one of Maui's liveliest nightclubs, with a rotating schedule of DJs, live music and Latin-dance nights. *1188 Makawao Ave, Makawao. Tel: (808) 572-0220. www.casanovamaui.com. Open: Wed, Fri, Sat 10pm–2am. Cover charge.*

SPORT AND LEISURE

Ekahi Tours

Offers a variety of guided van tours around Maui, including a sunrise trip up Haleakala. *60 Kanoa St, Wailuku. Tel: (808) 877-9775. www.ekahi.com*

Thompson Ranch

Family-owned cattle ranch offering guided horseback rides around the upcountry. *Middle Rd, Keokea. Tel: (808) 878-1910. www.thompsonranchmaui.com*

The east

ACCOMMODATION

Hotel Hana-Maui ★★★★

This secluded resort offers ocean- and mountain-view cottage rooms with private *lanais* and kitchenettes, but no televisions. On site is the award-winning Honua Spa, a fitness centre, two pools, tennis courts and an upscale fine-dining restaurant. *5031 Hana Hwy, Hana. Tel: (808) 248-8211. www.hotelhanamaui.com*

EATING OUT

Hana Ranch Restaurant ★★

Casual restaurant with a lunch buffet, burgers, pizza, ribs, pasta, salads and the like. A takeout counter offers cheaper options for those in a hurry.

Hana Hwy, Hana.
Tel: (808) 248-8255.
Open: Sun–Tue
11am–4pm, Wed–Sat
11am–4pm & 6–8.30pm.

SPORT AND LEISURE

Luana Spa Retreat

Choose from a wide variety of massages and bodywork therapies such as traditional Hawaiian, Swedish, reiki or shiatsu.

5050 Uakea Rd, Hana.
Tel: (808) 248-8855.
www.luanaspa.com

KAUAI

The east side

ACCOMMODATION

Hotel Coral Reef Resort ★★

This beachfront hotel, one of Kauai's oldest, has recently undergone a complete renovation. Besides a new sauna and pool, it now offers rooms and small suites with king-sized beds, air-conditioning and flat-screen TVs, and some with Jacuzzi tubs.

1516 Kuhio Hwy, Kapa`a.
Tel: (808) 822-4481. www.
hotelcoralreefresort.com

Kauai Inn ★★

Modest rooms with decent amenities and a small pool. Central location a mile (0.5km) past Kalapaki Beach makes it a good-value base for day-tripping around the island.

2430 Hulemalu Rd,
Lihu`e. Tel: (808) 245-
9000. www.kauai-inn.com

EATING OUT

Duane's Ono Char-Burger★

'Ono' means delicious, and Duane's burgers have been voted best on the island the last few years running. Choose from a dozen different styles of burger; there's also a veggie burger, and fish and chicken sandwiches.

4–4350 Kuhio Hwy,
Anahola.
Tel: (808) 822-9181.
Open: Mon–Sat
10am–6pm, Sun
11am–6pm.

Small Town Coffee Co.★

A favourite local café with great coffees and teas, pastries, sandwiches and free wi-fi. Local musicians play several nights per week.

4–1495 Kuhio Hwy,
Kapa`a. Tel: (808) 821-
1604. www.
smalltowncoffee.com.
Open: Mon–Thur 6am–
9pm, Fri–Sat 6am–10pm,
Sun 6am–6pm.

Olympic Cafe ★–★★

An airy upstairs diner with a huge menu and portions to match, featuring a great selection of omelettes, burgers, wraps, salads, pasta, and fish, beef and chicken mains.

1354 Kuhio Hwy, Kapa`a.
Tel: (808) 822-5825.
Open: Sun–Thur 7am–
9pm, Fri–Sat 7am–10pm.

Blossoming Lotus ★★

This spectacular vegan restaurant recently earned the title of Best Restaurant on Kauai from the *Honolulu Advertiser*. The 'world fusion' menu offers delicious dishes from Asian, European and American cuisines.

4504 Kukui St, Kapa`a.

Tel: (808) 822-7678.
www.blossominglotus.com.
Open: 5–9.30pm.

**Gaylord's at
Kilohana ★★★**
European fine dining
combines with Hawaiian
influences in this elegant
(and excellent)
restaurant on the
Kilohana plantation. The
wine list is extensive.
Also offers lunch and a
breakfast buffet.
3–2087 Kaumuali`i Hwy
(Hwy 50), Lihu`e. Tel:
(808) 245-9593.
www.gaylordskauai.com.
Open: Mon–Sat 7.45–
9.45am, 11am–3pm &
5–9pm, Sun 7.45am–
3pm & 5–9pm.

**The south shore and
the west**
ACCOMMODATION
Kiahuna Plantation ★★
Huge beach resort with a
prime beachfront location
and all the amenities.
Offers modern, self-
contained one- or two-
bedroom condo units with
private lanais. Best
discounts online; bookings
through both Outrigger
and Castle Resorts.
2253 Po`ipu Rd, Po`ipu.
Tel: Outrigger (800) 688-

7444, Castle Resorts (800)
367-5004.
www.outrigger.com,
www.castleresorts.com

**Waimea Plantation
Cottages ★★**
One of Hawaii's most
unusual properties, with
several dozen 1900s-era
plantation workers'
cottages, all self-contained
and individually
decorated in appealing
rustic style. Book well in
advance. The on-site
restaurant has Kauai's
only microbrewery.
9400 Kaumuali`i Hwy,
Waimea. Tel: (808) 338-
1625. www.
waimeaplantation.com

EATING OUT
Hanapepe Café ★/★★
Friendly restaurant and
bakery with a popular
lunch menu of gourmet
vegetarian and fish dishes,
such as vegetable focaccia
and a garden burger.
Friday-night live music.
3830 Hanepepe Rd,
Hanapepe.
Tel: (808) 335-5011.
Open: Mon–Thur
7am–3pm, Fri 11am–2pm
& 6–9pm. Closed: Sat,
Sun. Dinner reservations
recommended.

**Roy's Po`ipu Bar &
Grill ★★**
Celebrity Japanese chef
Roy Yamaguchi created
this lively gourmet
restaurant with an
eclectic 'Hawaiian
Fusion' menu famous for
fish and seafood and his
signature chocolate
soufflé dessert.
2360 Kiahuna Plantation
Dr, Koloa.
Tel: (808) 742-5000.
www.roysrestaurant.com.
Open: 5.30–9.30pm.
Bookings essential.

SPORT AND LEISURE
Captain Andy's
Catamaran and
snorkelling trips to the
Na Pali coast, including a
sunset dinner sail.
Waimea. Tel: (808) 335-
2719. www.napali.com

Poipu Bay Golf Course
Top-notch coastal course
that hosts the yearly PGA
Grand Slam tournament.
2250 Ainako St, Koloa.
Tel: (800) 858-6300.
www.poipubaygolf.com

Seasport Divers
Scuba-diving and
snorkelling trips to over
a dozen locations around
Kauai. Also has a branch
in Kapa`a.

Po`ipu. Tel: (808) 742-9303.
www.seasportdivers.com

The north coast
ACCOMMODATION
Hanalei Colony Resort ★★
Self-contained two-bedroom condo apartments with private *lanais*, on-site yoga and wellness spa and a highly rated Mediterranean restaurant.
Kuhio Hwy, Ha`ena.
Tel: (808) 826-6235.
www.hcr.com

Princeville Resort ★★★★
Opulent hotel resort overlooking Hanalei Bay. Discounts available online if you join their free 'preferred guest' club.
5300 Ka Huku Rd, Princeville.
Tel: (800) 826-9066.
www.princevillehotel hawaii.com

EATING OUT
Polynesia Café ★
Popular café with a wide selection of salads, burgers, and meat, fish and vegetarian dishes from American, Asian and Mexican cuisines. Fresh local ice cream, too.
Ching Young Village, Hanalei.
Tel: (808) 826-1999.
www.polynesiacafe.com.
Open: 8am–9pm.

ENTERTAINMENT
Sushi Blues
This popular local Japanese restaurant offers live jazz music most nights from 8.30pm till late.
Ching Young Village, Hanalei.
Tel: (808) 826-9701.
www.sushiandblues.com.
Open: Mon–Thur noon–3.30pm & daily 6–10pm.

SPORT AND LEISURE
Hanalei Day Spa
Yoga classes and a variety of treatments like the traditional Hawaiian *lomi-lomi*, shiatsu or a warm oil massage. Walk-ins welcome.
Hanalei Colony Resort, Ha`ena. Tel: (808) 826-6621. www. hanaleidayspa.com. Open: Mon–Sat 10am–6pm, Sun by appointment.

MOLOKAI AND LANAI
Molokai
ACCOMMODATION
Hotel Molokai ★★
Slightly retro hotel featuring rooms and suites in two-storey beachfront cottages. Open-air restaurant with live music and entertainment nightly.
Kamehameha V Hwy, Kaunakakai.
Tel: (808) 553-5347.
www.hotelmolokai.com

Ke Nani Kai ★★
Individually owned, self-contained one-bedroom (sleeping four) and two-bedroom (sleeping six) condos for rent, with a swimming pool and two tennis courts on-site. You can book through the Ke Nani Kai office or find some unit owners' websites with a quick online search.
50 Kepuhi Pl, Kaluako`i.
Tel: (808) 552-0945.
www.kenanikai.com

Molokai Ranch ★★
Rustic-styled luxury rooms with all mod cons at the clifftop Lodge, or canvas 'tentalows' with two comfortable bedrooms and private open-air bathrooms down at the Beach Village. Full complement of tours and activities.
Maunaloa.

Tel: (808) 660-2848.
www.molokairanch.com

Molokai Shores ★★
Shorefront
condominiums with
fully equipped, self-
contained one- and two-
bedroom apartments
with ocean-view *lanais*,
a swimming pool and
manicured lawns with
picnic tables and BBQ
grills (but no restaurant).
Kamehameha V Hwy,
Kaunakakai. Tel: (808)
553-5954/922-9700.
www.marcresorts.com

Pu`u O Hoku Ranch ★★
Two rustic, self-contained
guest cottages (two- and
four-bedroom) with
full kitchens offer
comfortable seclusion
at the eastern end of
the island.
Kamehameha V Hwy.
Tel: (808) 558-8109.
www.puuohoku.com

EATING OUT
Molokai Pizza Café ★
Popular family restaurant
with surprisingly good
pizza, as well as
sandwiches, chicken, ribs
and fresh fish specials,
and Mexican food on
Wednesdays. Takeout
also available.

Kaunakakai Place, Wharf
Rd, Kaunakakai. Tel:
(808) 553-3288. Open:
Mon–Thur 10am–10pm,
Fri & Sat 10am–11pm,
Sun 11am–10pm.

Outpost Natural Foods★
Small wholefood
supermarket with a
vegetarian lunch
counter and smoothie
and juice bar.
70 Maka`ena Pl,
Kaunakakai. Tel: (808)
553-3377. Open: Mon–
Thur 9am–6pm, Fri
9am–4pm, Sun 10am–
5pm. Closed: Sat.

Hula Shores ★★
Hotel Molokai's friendly,
open-air restaurant and
lounge, with live music
nightly, barbecue buffet
on Sundays, and crafts
fair and torch-lighting
ceremony on 'Aloha
Fridays'.
Hotel Molokai,
Kaunakakai.
Tel: (808) 553-5347.
www.hotelmolokai.com.
Open: 6am–9pm (kitchen).

The Lodge at Molokai
Ranch ★★★
The Maunaloa Room
offers hearty, home-style
American and
continental dishes for
breakfast and lunch,

while the Paniolo Lounge
has salads, sandwiches
and *pupus* for lunch on
its open-air verandah.
Maunaloa. Tel: (808)
660-2848.
www.molokairanch.com.
Open: 7am–9pm.

ENTERTAINMENT
Maunaloa Town
Cinemas
Modern, three-screen
cinema offering first-run
movies.
Maunaloa. Tel: (808)
552-2616.

SPORT AND LEISURE
Kaluako`i Golf Course
Ted Robinson designed
this highly rated,
ocean-front 18-hole
course whose slogan
is 'no waiting'.
Kaluako`i.
Tel: (808) 552-0255.
www.molokairanch.com

Molokai Fish & Dive
Offers scuba, snorkelling,
whale watching,
kayaking, bike tours,
hikes, horseback rides
and cultural tours.
63 Ala Malama St,
Kaunakakai.
Tel: (808) 553-5926.
www.
molokaifishanddive.com

Molokai Flower Farm

Friendly and knowledgeable flower farmer Kalani Pruet offers waterfall hikes (fresh fruit smoothies included) and tours of his home-grown heliconias and gingers. Accommodation is also available in a raised yurt.
Halawa Valley. Tel: (808) 336-1149. Email: kalanipruet@yahoo.com. www.molokaiflowers.com

Lanai

ACCOMMODATION

Hotel Lanai ★★

Ten quaint rooms and a guest cottage, all with plantation-style décor.
828 Lanai Ave. Tel: (808) 565-7211. www.hotellanai.com

The Lodge at Ko`ele (Four Seasons Resort) ★★★

A sumptuous, inland resort evoking a European country manor house, with a Greg Norman-designed golf course, spa, horseback tours and several restaurants with Italian, Pacific Rim and other cuisines, including those at sister resort Manele Bay.
One Keomoku Hwy. Tel:
(808) 565-4000. www. fourseasons.com/koele

Manele Bay Hotel (Four Seasons Resort) ★★★★

A lavish beach resort, featuring a golf course (designed by Jack Nicklaus), spa, tour activities, fine dining and high levels of attentive service.
One Manele Bay Road. Tel: (808) 565-2000. www.fourseasons.com/ manelebay

EATING OUT

Except for the fine dining at the two resorts, Lana`i City's food options can all be found around Dole Park.

Pele's Other Garden ★/★★

Features deli-style sandwiches, pizza and burritos for lunch and a bistro-style Italian menu for dinner. Also has a small healthfood store, and picnic baskets are available for ordering.
Houston and 8th Sts. Tel: (808) 565-9628. Open: Mon–Sat 9.30am– 3pm & 5–9pm.

Henry Clay's Rotisserie ★★★

Highly rated fine Cajun dining from the
eponymous New Orleans-native chef, using local ingredients like venison and seafood.
Hotel Lanai, 828 Lanai Ave. Tel: (808) 565-7211. Open: 5.30–9pm.

ENTERTAINMENT

Most options are to be found at the Four Seasons resorts.

Lanai Playhouse

A small, modern cinema with two shows per night Tue–Sun, and occasional matinees.
Lanai Ave & 7th St. Tel: (808) 565-7500.

SPORT AND LEISURE

Adventure Lanai Eco-center

Guided jeep and ATV tours, ocean kayaking, biking, hiking and PADI scuba.
Tel: (808) 565-7373. www.adventurelanai.com

Trilogy Excursions

Ocean tours around Lanai and Maui, including sailing, diving, snorkelling, dolphin-spotting and whale-watching.
Tel: (888) 225-MAUI, (808) 661-4743. www.sailtrilogy.com

Index

Acknowledgements

Thomas Cook wishes to thank ALISON LEMER for the loan of the photographs reproduced in this book, to whom copyright in the photographs belongs, except the following:

WORLD PICTURES/PHOTOSHOT 1

For CAMBRIDGE PUBLISHING MANAGEMENT LTD:
Project editor: Karen Beaulah
Typesetter: Trevor Double
Proofreader: Jan McCann
Indexer: Karolin Thomas

SEND YOUR THOUGHTS TO
BOOKS@THOMASCOOK.COM

We're committed to providing the very best up-to-date information in our travel guides and constantly strive to make them as useful as they can be. You can help us to improve future editions by letting us have your feedback. If you've made a wonderful discovery on your travels that we don't already feature, if you'd like to inform us about recent changes to anything that we do include, or if you simply want to let us know your thoughts about this guidebook and how we can make it even better – we'd love to hear from you.

Send us ideas, discoveries and recommendations today and then look out for your valuable input in the next edition of this title.

Emails to the above address, or letters to Travellers Series Editor, Thomas Cook Publishing, PO Box 227, Unit 9, Coningsby Road, Peterborough PE3 8SB, UK.

Please don't forget to let us know which title your feedback refers to!